ETHAN ALLEN
AND THE GREEN MOUNTAIN BOYS

ETHAN ALLEN
AND THE
GREEN MOUNTAIN
BOYS

by **SLATER BROWN**

Illustrated by **WILLIAM MOYERS**

RANDOM HOUSE · NEW YORK

JB
A

3-8-57

CONTENTS

ETHAN ALLEN
AND THE GREEN MOUNTAIN BOYS

1

Gods of the Hills

It was a green and pleasant land. The mountains stood peacefully against the sky. The valleys lay quietly mothering their brooks and rivers. No human blood stained the soil. The Indians had never made it their battleground and the French and Indian War had passed it by. But now the peaceful territory called the "Grants" was torn by a bitter struggle for ownership.

The Grants in 1765 was the region that we now call Vermont. It was bounded, as Vermont is today, by the Connecticut River on the east and by Lake Champlain on the west. Through its center run the Green Mountains like a good, stiff backbone—the sort of backbone Vermonters have never been afraid to show in a fight.

New Hampshire to the east of the Grants and New York to the west of it both claimed the territory as their own. Before they became states they were royal provinces. The land they occupied had been deeded over by kings of England who had only vague ideas about boundaries and even vaguer ideas about the geography of North America. As a result, many provinces had quarrels with their next-door neighbors over boundary lines. They were the same sort of quarrels farmers have over where a fence should run or where a wood lot ends. Disputes over boundary lines are one of the most ancient causes of bad blood between neighbors.

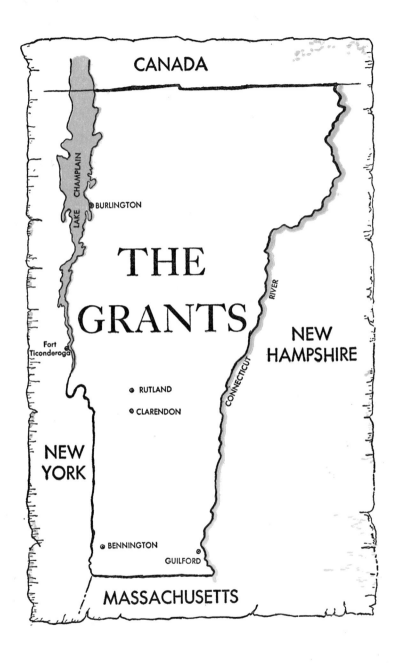

About the year 1770, there was bad blood between the two royal provinces of New York and New Hampshire. The New Yorkers felt they had a legal right to all the land up to the Connecticut River. They based their claim on the fact that this was the boundary called for in the deed King Charles the Second had given to his brother, the Duke of York.

The province of New Hampshire, on the other hand, claimed that its western boundaries should extend along an imaginary line running twenty miles east of and parallel to the Hudson River. This imaginary line marked the western limits of Massachusetts. As New Hampshire had once been a part of Massachusetts, it saw no reason why its own boundary should not run along a similar line.

So the fight over these overlapping claims, the fight over this green and pleasant land, became a bitter struggle for ownership.

Perhaps it wouldn't have become so bitter a struggle if it had been only a legal one. Other provinces had settled their boundary disputes in the courts without bloodshed. But the fight between New Hampshire and New York was a clash over human rights rather than legal ones. It was, in fact, a clash between two different ways of living.

One of these ways of living was a very old one and had been imported unchanged from England. It was the ancient landowning system of feudalism. Under this system farmers did not own the land on which they lived. They only rented it from big landowners who had the privilege of moving them out whenever they chose to do so. Tenants could not leave the farms to their widows or children when they died, yet their heirs were bound to pay "perpetual rent" to the landlords. Today these tenant farmers would be called peons. They were not free men, for they did not even have the right to vote in public elections.

The other way of life we might call the Yankee or American way. It had been imported only as a seed from the Old Country. But in the rocky soil of New England the seed had struck root and it grew into a new way of living. It grew into a society that gave the common man free schools for his children, town meetings, and the right to vote as he saw fit. But most important, at least for the settlers in the Grants, it gave a poor farmer the right to purchase and own the land he had cleared, plowed, harrowed, and planted—the land that supported and fed his family.

The first of these two systems, the feudal one, held its sway in New York. The other system, the Yankee one, was common to all of New England. And the two systems clashed on the battleground, the no man's land of the Grants.

The fight started in 1763 when the Peace of Paris, ending the French and Indian War, opened up the Grants to settlement by English colonists. The governors of New Hampshire and New York, both claiming the territory, began selling townships there.

8

A township was about six miles square. The governor of New York sold townships to his powerful landowning friends for two hundred or so pounds a piece. That was almost a thousand dollars, a high price to pay for wild land in those days. The governor of New Hampshire was a little less greedy. He asked only twenty pounds and sold the townships off to real-estate promoters. These in turn subdivided the land and sold parcels at reasonable prices to small farmers.

Brawny pioneers, mostly from western Connecticut, began buying the land and moving into the Grants with their families. But when they had cleared away the trees, planted their Indian corn among the tree stumps, and built their log cabins, they found that the rich New York landlords claimed the land for themselves. Sheriffs began arriving with imposing looking documents that they shook in the settlers' faces, ordering them to clear out of the territory and take their wives and their children with them.

The shouting and the threats may have frightened the settlers' children but it didn't frighten the settlers, or their wives, either. Folks who had plowed their fields with a musket handy to fight off prowling Indians weren't the kind to shake in their boots at the sight of a sheriff from New York. But it worried them. They didn't want to lose their farms and they didn't want to see tenant farming and serfdom come into the Grants.

The real trouble began in the township of Bennington in the southern end of the Grants. The New York landlords who laid claim to this township were outraged at seeing Connecticut settlers squatting on what they considered their land. But unable to move the settlers out with threats and bluster, the New York landlords decided to make a test case of it in the courts.

It was at this point that Ethan Allen stepped onto the scene to champion the cause of his fellow townsmen.

Ethan Allen, besides being one of the smartest

men in the Grants, was one of the tallest, too. The flintlock he carried was sixty-nine inches long, but it was almost a foot shorter than Ethan himself. He was as strong as a young bull and he had a fine set of white teeth. It was said that he could pick up a hundred-pound sack of salt with these fine white teeth and flip it over his shoulder. But it was because of his gift of gab and his Connecticut shrewdness that the settlers asked him to manage the defense of their interests in the court at Albany.

Ethan at once engaged a smart lawyer from New Haven. His name was Jared Ingersoll and he had for some years handled affairs for the Connecticut Province in London. He and his friends, like most New Englanders, sympathized with Ethan's clients and were ready to defend them.

It was a lost cause. All the members of the court were New York landlords with large claims to the land in question. And they didn't feel like deciding against themselves. So the hearing in Al-

ETHAN
ALLEN

The flintlock he carried was 69 inches long.

bany, which lasted only a few minutes, ended with the judges deciding against the settlers. They were ordered to move out of the land they had bought from the New Hampshire governor unless they would rebuy it from New York.

After the hearing two of the Yorkers came to the tavern in Albany where Ethan Allen was staying. One of them was the attorney general of New York, the other was a Yorker lawyer. The lawyer's name was James Duane but he was known as "Old Swivel-Eye." He had got this unpleasant nickname from his ability to see everyone in a courtroom without moving his head. He and the attorney general came to the tavern to look Ethan over and make him a proposition.

The proposition was a disgraceful one. If Ethan would persuade his fellow townsmen to move out of the Grants peacefully, the Yorkers would award Ethan a large tract of land.

Ethan angrily rejected the proposal.

The Yorkers then turned to threats.

Ethan angrily rejected the proposal.

"The people settled in the Grants," thundered the attorney general as he thumped the table where the three men were sitting, "might just as well make the best terms they can with their rightful landlords. We have might on our side, and you know that might often prevails against right."

Ethan thought over this remark. He knew, as he sat there, that many answers could be made to the threat and he thought them over, one by one. Then he finished drinking his cider and set the empty flagon down on the table.

"Gentlemen," he drawled, as he prepared to utter the remark that loyal Vermonters, it is said, are still taught in their cradles, "the gods of the hills are not the gods of the valleys."

The attorney general and Old Swivel-Eye sat looking puzzled. Ethan's shot had gone over their heads and they admitted as much.

"What do you mean, Mr. Allen," Old Swivel-Eye asked, "that the gods of the hills are not the gods of the valleys?"

At this point Ethan stood up. He buttoned his fawnskin jacket and reached for his bearskin hat.

"If you will accompany me to the hill in Bennington," he said, "the sense will be made clear."

Then, leaving the two Yorkers to puzzle over what he had said, he climbed on his horse and set out at a gallop for home.

If the Yorkers had dared to follow him there, they wouldn't have puzzled long over what Ethan meant. For the gods of the hills, up Bennington way at least, were beginning to come out of the woods. And though they didn't look much like gods in their buckskin shirts and coonskin hats, they were dead shots when it came to using a flintlock. Also, they had some pretty obstinate ideas about the rights of a free man in a free country. The Yorkers took to calling them "The Bennington Mob" and jeered at them. But the name these young gods of the hills took for themselves was the Green Mountain Boys. And they were proud of the title.

2

The First Encounter

A rough-and-tumble lot were the Green Mountain Boys. They had come from the Connecticut towns of New Milford, Sharon, Salisbury, and Litchfield. Ethan himself had been born in Litchfield in 1738 when it was still a frontier town as wild and woolly as any frontier town out West. It consisted mostly of log cabins then, for the big white houses with their massive chimneys hadn't yet sprung up around the Village Green. And the men who lived there were, like all pioneers, quick on the trigger and eager to try out new land.

They had moved to the Grants, bringing their families, their axes and iron kettles, their flintlocks, and a determination to stay put. When Ethan returned from Albany with the news that the royal court had decided against them, they were quick to follow Ethan in organizing a resistance.

Ethan himself had long before realized the need for a compact body of fighters in the event the powerful landlords of New York carried out their threats. He had seen what happened when farmers tried to fight New York without being properly organized.

On Quaker Hill in New York, a tenant farmer named William Prendergast had led a revolt of more than a thousand tenant farmers against their landlords. The tenants were sick of being denied ownership of the land they lived on and were eager to throw off the old feudal system that kept them impoverished. But they were not properly organized nor properly armed. When a company of British regulars was sent against them, the revolt collapsed.

Prendergast was thrown into prison, along with fifty of his followers. He was charged with treason for raising a rebellion against His Majesty, George the Third, King of England. This, of course, was a capital offense and Prendergast faced hanging. Old Swivel-Eye Duane handled the prosecution and did it so expertly that Prendergast was sentenced not only to be hanged but to be drawn and quartered as well.

Prendergast would certainly have ended his days in four pieces if his Quaker wife, Mehitabel Wing, hadn't saved his life. A brave and energetic woman, Mehitabel dashed to New York City on horseback and managed to win a reprieve from the governor. She did more. She did not rest until she had obtained a pardon for her husband from King George himself.

Ethan had probably heard Prendergast's story at first hand. He often visited Quaker Hill and it is likely that he heard the story of the revolt from the leader himself. Ethan was well aware of the danger he faced if he led a fight against the big landlords and the powerful province of New York. He had no desire to see his Green Mountain Boys tossed into jail, or hanged, drawn and quartered. Perhaps, too, he didn't wholly trust his own wife's ability to get him a reprieve from the governor or a pardon from King George. Mary Brownson, whom he had married, was a good talker but she was no Quaker firebrand like Mehitabel Wing.

Ethan at once set to work organizing his Green Mountain Boys. He planned to have a band of fighters who wouldn't turn tail at the first sight of a British redcoat or a Yorker sheriff. He picked his men with care. After assuming the high-sounding title of Colonel Commandant, he appointed his captains. He soon had a group of fighting men he could trust. There was Robert

He had a group of fighting men he could trust.

Cochran, a swashbuckling sort of a fellow. And Remember Baker, Ethan's cousin, a tough, hot-tempered Yankee but an expert woodsman and hunter. Seth Warner, mild tempered and friendly, could shoot the eye out of a squirrel at fifty paces. Peleg Sunderland, who had hunted every hill and valley in the Grants, "feared neither bear or Tory." Also picked as captains were Ethan's brother Heman, and Gideon Warren. Then there was Jonas Fay, the "doctor and surrugeon," as the old records describe him, son of the owner of the Catamount Tavern.

Headquarters for the Green Mountain Boys was the Catamount Tavern in Bennington. It was a huge building for those days with plenty of room for meetings. Many an evening before the trouble in the Grants began, Ethan had sprawled happily in its taproom before a roaring fire, telling tall tales of his prowess in the woods. How he had run down a herd of deer on his own long legs. Or how one bitterly cold night he had become lost in the woods and, marking out a great circle in the snow, had tramped round and round it until dawn to keep from freezing to death.

As headquarters for the "Bennington Mob," the tavern was well named. Before its front door stood a twenty-five foot pole atop of which perched a large, stuffed "cat-of-the-mountains," or wildcat. Its significance lay in the fierce snarl on its face and the direction in which it was snarling. It was snarling toward the west, toward New York, and it looked as if it meant business. The catamount meant that if the Yorkers started coming into the Grants with any hope of evicting the settlers or imposing their system of tenant farming, they would have to tangle with a pack of wildcats first. And a well organized pack, too.

(The old building with its great chimneys and its wide door no longer stands. Gone is the stuffed catamount, too. But in their place there now stands a tall shaft of granite on which perches a catamount of bronze.)

Having appointed his captains and enlisted all the young men he could find, Ethan sent scouts to watch the New York trails. He selected others to spread the alarm if and when the Yorkers started coming. And he saw to it that everyone was supplied with powder, lead bullets and, in case of need, a "good tomahawk." Ethan had no intention of making Prendergast's mistake of being ill-armed.

The Yorkers were not long in coming. The court's decision in favor of the New York landlords had given them the right they thought they needed. Also, they imagined that they had the might, too. So Sheriff Ten Eyck of Albany called together a posse of several hundred men, armed them and set out for Bennington to enforce the law and make a sorry example of one of the settlers.

The settler the Yorkers had chosen, for they already had had trouble with him, was Jim Breakenridge. He was a resolute old farmer and he was in no mood to surrender his property without a fight. Neither were the Green Mountain Boys in a mood to see him run off his farm. And when scouts reported that a posse was approaching, the call for arms went out.

As one man the Green Mountain Boys came

They started for the Breakenridge place at a gallop.

out of their hayfields and grimly unslung their
flintlocks from hooks above their mantlepieces.
Then they mounted their old plow horses and
started for the Breakenridge place at a smart
gallop.

Their commander, Ethan Allen, wasn't present.
He was off gunning for a Yorker surveyor up
north near Rutland. But he had left instructions
and his captains took over. The Breakenridge
house was quickly turned into a fortress. Loop-

holes were chopped through the log walls and soon the place was bristling with guns. Scattered through the hayfields and corn lot sat dozens of young men with loaded fowling pieces across their knees. By the time Sheriff Ten Eyck and his army reached the scene, they had begun to realize that evicting old Jim Breakenridge from his farm wasn't going to be an easy matter. The Green Mountain catamount was snarling and baring his claws.

A quarter mile from the Breakenridge place, Sheriff Ten Eyck halted. He sent a couple of officers to parley with Breakenridge. The old farmer came out of his house. While the Boys inside kept the Yorkers covered, Breakenridge announced that he had no intention of surrendering his farm. He was, he declared, under the protection of the town of Bennington and the town of Bennington was not afraid of tangling with the sheriff's troops.

Having delivered his speech, Jim Breakenridge

lighted his pipe, went back into his house and slammed the door behind him.

The Sheriff's two emissaries were taken aback. Silently they stood contemplating the house bristling with guns. They looked toward the hayfield and saw a lot of rough-looking young men standing around chewing straws and holding flintlocks carelessly in the crooks of their arms. They looked toward the corn lot and saw other young men sitting on stumps with guns standing ready between their knees. They glanced up at a ridge overlooking the house and saw forty or so men leaning against the trees and gazing down sorrowfully at them.

The two emissaries exchanged glances and without a word hustled back to their commander.

Sheriff Ten Eyck's face grew red as he listened to their report. He whipped his sword from its scabbard and waved it angrily above his head.

"Forward march!" he shouted.

Still full of fight and determination, the Sheriff's army started off gallantly toward the Breakenridge place. Sheriff Ten Eyck marched proudly at the head, flourishing his sword. But as his gallant army caught sight of the force gathered to oppose them, they began to have second thoughts about fighting. By twos and threes they drifted off thoughtfully into the woods and surrounding fields. When the Sheriff reached Breakenridge's front gate and whirled around to order his brave soldiers to prepare for an attack, he found to his dismay that only twenty men were left.

However, the Sheriff was not to be hindered by the desertion of his army. Even though he had only twenty men, he was determined to enforce the law. He marched up to the front door and drew the writ of ejectment from his pocket. Putting on his spectacles, he read it in a loud voice. Then he demanded in the name of the law and His Royal Majesty George the Third that Jim Breakenridge open his door and peacefully depart.

No response came from inside the house. One

The Sheriff was determined to enforce the law.

of the guns poking through a loophole moved a few inches to the right as an invisible marksman drew a bead on the Sheriff's beaver hat.

The Sheriff waited a moment and angrily shouted his order again. Again there was dead silence from within. In the hayfield a few of the men moved uneasily.

"Smash down the door!" the Sheriff roared.

Two of the Sheriff's men started toward it, the butts of their muskets raised. But at the same instant the men on the ridge, in the corn lot, and in the hayfield quietly raised their guns. They took careful aim at the Sheriff's men and stood waiting with their guns cocked.

Perhaps the Sheriff heard the click of the hammers as the Green Mountain Boys cocked their trusty flintlocks. Perhaps the two soldiers with the raised muskets noticed that the guns from inside the house were following their progress toward the door. At any rate they halted.

The Sheriff barked out an order. But it was not an order to keep going. It was an order to retreat.

The Yorkers all retreated rapidly, led by the Sheriff himself. Without stopping, they hastily made their way through the woods back to Albany. The Sheriff did not come across the rest of his posse. And for a good reason. The posse had a head start of an hour and hadn't wasted any time hitting the trail for home!

We don't know what Sheriff Ten Eyck said to his governor, or what the governor said to him. It isn't in the record. We only know that he probably reported that the Grants was an armed camp and ready to resist any efforts of the Yorkers to take away the land and settle it with their own browbeaten tenants. For some reason, the settlers in the Grants didn't fancy the fine old English feudal system that the Yorkers were trying to hand them on a platter.

3

Twigs of the Wilderness

Ethan, as we have seen, wasn't present to see the Yorker sheriff's feeble attempt to toss crusty Jim Breakenridge and his family off their farm. He was up near Rutland gunning for a Yorker surveyor named William Cockburn.

Rutland is about sixty miles north of Bennington. That seems like a long journey to make on foot through rough country in order to catch a surveyor. But it was part of Ethan's carefully laid plan.

Ethan knew from experience that if the Yorker landlords were to be kept out for good, they must be kept out from the very beginning. He realized that once they had got a foothold, once they had put a few of their tenant farmers on the land, the royal province of New York would be obliged to protect them. And Ethan knew that the protection would come in the shape of British regulars.

Ethan had no illusions about the effectiveness of a body of untrained men, no matter how brave they were, against a well-equipped army. He knew how easily the British regulars had smashed the Prendergast rebellion. He had perhaps seen with his own eyes the murderous work they had done along the New York-Massachusetts boundary where they had burned barns and houses, destroyed crops, driven the farmers off their land.

Though he realized that he must be ready to fight them if they came, Ethan did not want to see the British troops march into the Grants. He knew it would mean bloodshed and he wished to avoid that as long as he could. The Yorkers, therefore, must be given as little excuse as possible to call upon British troops for help. And there would be little excuse if Yorker settlers were prevented from coming into the Grants. Ethan was determined to keep them out and to squelch any attempt of the Yorker landlords to get even a toehold. And to this purpose Ethan used all his native wits in a shrewd campaign of threat and bluster.

Some folks, even loyal Vermonters, tired of hearing Ethan praised beyond measure and forgetting his tactics, have sometimes called him a loud-mouthed braggart, a blowhard, a "four-flusher." They have often quoted him as making such hair-raising remarks as "We shall make a hell of his house and burn him in it," or that he "would lay all Durham in ashes and leave every person in it a corpse."

Perhaps Ethan talked this way, though these oft-quoted remarks, it must be observed, are quotations from affidavits drawn up by his enemies. However, there is no doubt that Ethan on occasion did threaten and bluster. And often what he said was pure bluff. But bluffing can be effective in war and every smart general has used it.

Nevertheless the Yorkers soon came to realize that most of Ethan's threats were real and that he was determined to keep their feudal system of landowning out of his own precincts.

Ethan knew better than most of his fellow townsmen what the feudal system meant to the poor farmer. When he was still a boy his father had moved the family from Litchfield to Cornwall. Cornwall was only a few miles from the New York line, close enough for Ethan to see the feudal system in operation. And it made him realize what might have happened to his brothers and sisters if they had been living under New York rule when his father died.

Ethan came of a big family. He was the oldest of eight children. He had five younger brothers—Heman, Heber, Levi, Zimri, Ira (the names straight out of the Bible)—and two sisters named Lydia and Lucy. When Ethan was eighteen his father died suddenly and was buried in the lot behind the house. Ethan's mother inherited the farm and the family continued living there.

This wouldn't have been possible under the Yorker way of life. Across the line a tenant farmer's widow could inherit nothing but her husband's debts and obligations. And if she and her brood weren't able to continue the rent, out they would go, bag and baggage, even though the old man had put a lifetime of toil into the place he had called his home.

Even as a young man of eighteen, Ethan had

mulled over the injustice of a landowning system that prevented a man from handing on to his children property that he had perhaps carved out of the wilderness with his own hands. Ethan's alert and inquiring mind had led him to do much reading on the subject and on many other subjects, too. Indeed he had shown so much interest in reading that plans had been made to send him to Yale College. But the sudden death of his father put an end to that idea. With the strength of character Ethan always showed, he put his broad shoulders to the wheel at home. But he still managed to continue his reading and to ask sharp questions.

It was about this time that Ethan came under the influence of a young doctor who had moved to Amenia, just across the line in New York. Like so many free spirits of his time, Dr. Young, who had just been graduated from Yale, called himself a Deist. A Deist believed in God but refused to accept divine revelation. Deists in 1770 were regarded with horror by the devout, though many clergymen today would not find it necessary to leave the table if somebody like Dr. Young began talking. Under Dr. Young's influence Ethan became a Deist too. But we shouldn't let his religious convictions overshadow his other beliefs. For Dr. Young gave Ethan other ideas. They were ideas the doctor shared with the forefathers of this country—ideas that we find imbedded in the Declaration of Independence and in our Constitution.

One of Dr. Young's favorite slogans was "Life, Liberty and Property." This slogan, particularly its emphasis on the right of every man to own the property he lived on, made a deep impression on Ethan. All through his life he repeated it. The slogan appears in all his writings and he constantly used it when he spoke. In fact, he made the hills and Green Mountains ring with it.

Dr. Young himself never followed Ethan to the Green Mountains. He went to Boston where he became one of the leading patriots. He helped organize the Boston Tea Party, but he was not one of those who disguised themselves as Indians when the tea was dumped into Boston harbor.

Like Dr. Young, Ethan was never afraid of admitting openly what he believed in. If he was a Deist, he announced it. And when he believed in "Life, Liberty and Property" for his fellow citizens, he told folks that he did. Nor was he afraid of speaking out against the lack of real liberty in New York, the lack of town meetings there, the lack of free schools, the lack of freedom to own the land one lived on.

"I'd rather eat mouse meat," Ethan once said, "than live under New York."

From the very start, even before he owned a square foot of land in the Grants, Ethan did not want to see the old feudal system of New York spread anywhere else.

There was little danger of its spreading into Connecticut where Ethan had been raised. But in the open territory of the Grants, as we have seen, there was real danger. Ethan had fallen in love with the Green Mountain country when he had first seen it as a soldier during the French and Indian War. Later on he had explored it during one winter, living on venison and sleeping under a bearskin. Then when the first opportunity offered he had moved his young wife, Mary, and his children to the Grants. It became his home and, like the other settlers, he was ready to defend it with his life.

So with a firm determination to keep the Yorkers from ever getting a toehold, Ethan was always on the alert for the first danger signals of an invasion. When news was brought him that Surveyor Cockburn was running lines for the Yorkers up Rutland way, he called together some Green Mountain Boys and hot-footed it north.

Cockburn was surveying for Old Swivel-Eye

Duane. Duane had bought 48,000 acres from one of the more corrupt New York governors. Cockburn himself owned a large chunk of 30,000 acres and he was busy surveying both properties in preparation for moving in some Yorker tenants to settle them.

Arrived at the scene, Ethan and his Boys did not descend on the surveyor at once. Ethan wanted to feel out his opponents. If Cockburn and his men showed fight, he was ready to meet them. On the other hand, if they turned tail and ran at the first threat of violence, so much the better. Gathering his Boys together, Ethan dressed them up like Indians and let the word get out that he was on a "wolf hunt."

Settlers in the neighborhood, who had been alarmed at seeing Cockburn running lines across the land they claimed under New Hampshire patents, soon carried the news to the surveyor. They told him Ethan had boasted that he and his men would scalp Cockburn alive if he persisted in surveying that area.

"They've got tomahawks with them," the settlers said gloomily. "It looks like a scalping party."

"Who are the rascals?" Cockburn asked. "Don't they know I'm within my rights here?"

The settlers shrugged their shoulders, as if to say they hadn't heard much talk about Cockburn's rights. "One of them is a mighty big man," they said. "His name's Ethan Allen and he talks something fearful. Even had us scairt the way he and his men carried on back there in the woods."

Cockburn nervously inquired how many men Ethan had.

"Dozens. And Mr. Allen says more's acomin'. They're all rigged out like wild Injuns."

Cockburn stared suspiciously at the settlers. He didn't quite believe their story. Neither did he like to take any chances. Several days before one of the settlers had taken a few pot shots at

The Green Mountain Boys were dressed up like Indians.

his party and he didn't much care to fight a band
of wild Indians, particularly if they weren't real
ones. Running lines in the Grants, he realized,
wasn't the peaceful occupation he had thought it
was going to be. He would need an armed force
to protect him.

Biting his lip, he pocketed his compass and ordered his linesmen to roll up the chain. Then he
turned to the settlers.

"You can tell Mr. Allen," he said, "that I'll be back. And with guns."

The settlers nodded. Grinning at one another, they watched Cockburn and his men plod away through the woods toward New York. They hurried to tell Ethan what had happened.

Though he could easily have caught him, Ethan let Cockburn go. But other Yorker surveyors whom Ethan and his Boys caught later on when the fight got thicker didn't fare so well. When Ethan caught them redhanded running their lines in the Grants he gave them a form of punishment he called the "beech seal" or the "twigs of the wilderness."

Ethan may have named it in one of his lighthearted moments, but it was no light punishment to receive. The victim was stripped to the waist, tied to a tree, and then flogged with beech saplings cut on the spot by the Green Mountain Boys. Some of these whippings, even in an age when whippings and floggings were an accepted method of punishment, were far from gentle. And some of them might make our hair stand on end today.

There is no blinking the fact that Ethan Allen, Robert Cochran, Remember Baker and some of the other Green Mountain Boys were ruthless when they were aroused. But however brutal the whippings might seem to us, they made a surveyor think twice before he ventured into the Grants a second time. And that was their purpose.

The twigs of the wilderness and the beech seal weren't the only forms of punishment the Green Mountain Boys inflicted on stubborn opponents. Sometimes the punishment was meted out in a highly amusing manner.

Such was the case with Dr. Samuel Adams. Dr. Adams lived in Arlington, Vermont, and evidently had some strong ideas of his own. He held land under a New Hampshire title, but for some reason known only to himself, he began announcing that New Hampshire titles were illegal. It was his private opinion that settlers holding New

Hampshire titles should re-purchase them from the New Yorkers. He held forth on this subject so loudly that Ethan sent him a warning. If he valued his hide, he had better watch his tongue.

The noisy doctor kept on talking. Moreover he armed himself with a brace of pistols and announced that he would blast anyone who tried to silence him. Ethan thereupon dispatched a squad of Boys to bring the talkative doctor to headquarters at the Catamount Tavern.

The Boys caught the doctor napping. They grabbed him before he could bring his brace of pistols into play and hustled him down the road to Bennington. There, in front of the Catamount Tavern, he was brought before a Committee of Safety and given a hearing. The doctor had been so loud in his opinions that he could hardly deny the charges of disloyalty and he was found guilty.

Ethan himself pronounced the sentence. Doctor Adams was to be tied securely in a large and comfortable chair and then hauled to the top of

Dr. Adams was hauled to the top of the pole.

the twenty-five foot pole in front of the tavern. There he could hold forth to his heart's content under the grinning jaws of the stuffed catamount.

The sentence was immediately put into execution. To the cheers of the Bennington populace, the doctor was hoisted skyward in his chair. Then while the Green Mountain Boys drank his health and asked him how the royal province of New York looked from his lofty position, the doctor, blustering and fuming, was left suspended in mid-air for two hours.

Dr. Adams was one of the few pro-Yorkers who never learned his lesson. Later on he became a Tory and had to escape to Canada. But most of the doctor's friends soon learned that when Ethan talked about "Life, Liberty and Property" he meant what he said. It was becoming dangerous to argue with him.

4

Ethan Becomes an Outlaw

Sir William Tryon, Governor of New York and a big owner of land in the Grants, had been irritated by his sheriff's failure to evict Breakenridge. He had been angered by Ethan's successful bullying of surveyor William Cockburn. But now he was infuriated by the attack on old Dr. Adams.

He considered it downright rebellion on the part of the Green Mountain Boys.

For some reason he had come to believe that though the Bennington Mob might bedevil the Yorker officials, they wouldn't dare tackle any hard-boiled settlers. Particularly if the settlers happened to be rugged veterans of the French and Indian War. Thus when a group of these Indian fighters moved into the Grants near Rupert, began clearing the land and building themselves cabins, Tryon smilingly imagined that his royal province was at last getting a toehold in Ethan Allen's sacred preserves.

The Governor was again mistaken. He might have saved himself a lot of trouble had he taken the time to study a beehive. A highly organized hive of bees, united in a common bond and with their stingers on the alert, react quickly when an intrusion takes place. Even when a bee from another hive enters with the friendliest intentions and all the legal right in the world, he is lucky if he gets out of the alien hive all in one piece. The Green Mountain Boys shared with the bees this ungenerous attitude toward uninvited guests. Particularly when the guests came from New York.

The Yorker settlers had been at their task of opening up the land and building their cabins for a week or so when news of their activities reached Ethan at the Catamount. Ethan immediately raised the battle cry.

"We're going on a big wolf hunt!"

In the course of a few hours he had raised a large posse. This included his cousin Remember Baker and Robert Cochran, two of the toughest fighters in Bennington. They didn't take the time to dress up like wild Indians, but they took along their tomahawks and, with blood in their eyes, hit the trail for Rupert.

Rupert was more than thirty miles to the north,

but they made the trip in a day. The following morning they loaded their rifles, surrounded the settlement, and then walked in on the Rupert men. Caught unprepared, the Yorkers didn't have a chance to put up a fight. Ethan and his men herded them into a clearing. While some of the Boys kept them covered, the rest tore down the cabins, piled the logs in a heap and set them afire.

"We decided this morning," Ethan explained with a pleasant grin, "to offer a burnt sacrifice to the gods of the hills."

When the buildings had been destroyed and the last traces of the settlement erased, the Yorkers were speedily sent on their way. As they started off toward Albany Ethan shouted to them to tell their scoundrel of a governor that hundreds of loyal Hampshire men were armed and ready to battle anyone else who came to settle in the Grants.

"Tell him," Ethan shouted, "that we defy the governor, the New York council, the Assembly, and all the rest of New York, too. And if a Yorker constable tries to arrest any of my men we'll wring his neck. And if any Green Mountain Boy is lodged in an Albany jail we'll tear it down and set him free."

Fuming with wrath and with Ethan's threats ringing in their ears, the settlers returned to Albany. There under the promptings of lawyers they drew up affidavits describing their uncivilized treatment. We still can read these affidavits. Though they were drawn up by angry and prejudiced men who were in no condition to make trustworthy reports, we can be pretty certain that Ethan didn't mince his words.

Sir William read the men's affidavits, heard their story and then called his council together. Things had come to a pretty pass, he announced, when a mob led by a foul-mouthed ruffian could defy the royal province of New York. A stop must be put to it.

"Tell your governor," Ethan shouted, "that we defy him!"

But how? Governor Tryon deliberated on this thorny problem. He remembered Sheriff Ten Eyck's disgraceful failure to hold his posse together. He realized that many of his own subjects secretly sympathized with the Hampshire men in their fight to hold their land. His hands were tied. Until Ethan committed some act outrageous enough to warrant calling upon General Gage and his British regulars, Tryon could only threaten and bluster.

By advice of his council, Tryon issued a proclamation. It declared that Ethan, Baker and Cochran were outlaws and offered a reward for their arrest. Tryon hoped that even if his sheriffs found Ethan and his friends too tough to handle, some Yorker bullyboy might find the money attractive enough to take a chance. And, of course, there was always the possibility that some Green Mountain Boy might betray his leader.

As might have been expected by everyone but the bumbling Governor, Ethan and his Boys greeted the proclamation with rousing jeers. Then, to make their attitude clear to everyone, Ethan, Baker and Cochran issued a proclamation themselves. They offered a reward of twenty-five pounds for the arrest of attorney general Kempe and Old Swivel-Eye.

"Whereas," this burlesque proclamation began, "James Duane and John Kempe have by their menaces and threats greatly disturbed the public peace and repose of the honest peasants of Bennington . . ." Then the proclamation went on to say that anyone bringing these "common disturbers" to the Catamount Tavern would receive the reward offered. Ethan had the proclamation printed in Hartford, the three men signed it and posted it throughout the Grants.

The settlers were delighted by Ethan's mock proclamation in which he expressed his contempt for the Governor's authority, but they roared with laughter at Ethan's next exploit.

One night at the Catamount Tavern one of the Green Mountain Boys dared Ethan to post one of his proclamations across the line in New York. Ethan, who had never been known to refuse a dare, finished the cider he was drinking and banged his mug on the table.

"Across the line in New York!" he exclaimed.

58

"By the great lord Harry, I'll post one under the sheriff's own nose in Albany!"

True to his word, on the following morning Ethan climbed on his horse and rode straight into the heart of the city. Dismounting at the front door, he strode into Landlord Benedict's Tavern. Patrons fell back in alarm as the big man marched up to a table and flung down some coins. "A drink, landlord!" he shouted.

Quaking in his boots, for he had at once recognized the tall stranger, Landlord Benedict brought Ethan his drink. Ethan raised it above his head.

"To the Green Mountain Boys!" he roared.

Drinking it off in one swallow, he banged the empty flagon on the table. Then he strode across the taproom to the wall on which the placard announcing Tryon's reward for his arrest was posted. He ripped it from the wall and in its place posted his own offer for the arrest of Kempe and Duane. Then while the Yorkers stood pop-eyed with astonishment at his audacity, he marched out of the tavern, jumped on his horse and, waving his hat, clattered down the Albany streets toward home.

For weeks after, the Grants chuckled over the daring exploit. They admired Ethan's spunk, and particularly the playful way he treated the whole business. Leaders with a sense of humor are rare in any age or place, and Ethan's fellow townsmen recognized it as a good sign.

Though Governor Tryon's offer of a reward for the capture of the Green Mountain Boys wasn't taken seriously by Ethan, there was a Yorker justice of the peace who did take it seriously. His name was John Munro and he was acting agent for Duane and his hand-jobbing friends. Eager to curry favor with the Governor and to win the reward, he decided to kidnap Remember Baker, hustle him across the Hudson River and lodge him in the Albany jail where he could be held for trial.

Munro went about his plans cautiously. He

knew that with one false step he would have the Green Mountain Boys swarming around him like angry hornets. Moreover he knew that Baker alone could handle a half dozen Yorkers. Baker was tall and slim, but years of hunting had given his muscles the ruggedness of Vermont granite.

Having set a spy to watch Baker's house in Arlington, Munro waited until he was sure that Baker, his wife and his small son were sound asleep. Then with a gang of a dozen or so men he surrounded the house a few hours before sunrise. At a given signal, Munro and his men smashed down the door and caught Remember Baker in his nightshirt in bed.

'Member was no man to surrender without a fight, even if he had been caught in his nightshirt. He grabbed up an ax that stood handy and went after the Yorkers. His wife and his small son, being of good Yankee stock, went after them too. Soon the posse had its hands full. However, a blow from a cutlass lopped off 'Member's thumb. Wounded and bleeding, Baker tore upstairs, kicked out the clapboards under the eaves and jumped out. Unfortunately he landed in a snowdrift where he stuck. Floundering around there, he was easily captured.

Leaving Mrs. Baker and her stalwart son lying senseless on the floor, Munro and his men bundled Baker into a sleigh. They started triumphantly for Albany with their prize. On the way they gave Baker a good working over to quiet him down and teach him manners.

However, Munro had not counted on the fact that the Green Mountain Boys were ever on the alert for just such an occasion. One of Baker's neighbors, guessing what the uproar was about, dashed to Bennington on a horse and spread the alarm. In fifteen minutes a dozen Green Mountain Boys were cantering along the road in hot pursuit.

Taking a cross-cut, they reached the Hudson ferry before Munro and his kidnaping party arrived. Munro, congratulating himself on his successful exploit, had made the mistake of halting along the way for a brief rest. The Boys, backtracking, met his party at Sancoik, six miles from the Hudson ferry.

Though both groups were equally matched in number, Munro's men halted in dismay when they saw the Green Mountain Boys bearing down on them. Then like Sheriff Ten Eyck's posse they found urgent reasons for dashing off into the woods. Munro was left with his captive and two sheriffs.

Furious with his men for deserting him, Justice Munro saw his hopes for the reward go glimmering. He meekly surrendered his prisoner.

Remember Baker, weak from loss of blood and rough treatment, was hoisted upon a horse. With a Green Mountain Boy mounted behind to steady him in the saddle, he was galloped back to Bennington. The party reached there at two o'clock the following morning. In twenty-two hours Baker had covered sixty or more miles. Even for a

Remember Baker grabbed an ax and fought the Yorkers.

man in the pink of condition that was a lot of traveling.

The settlers in the Grants and the Green Mountain Boys never forgot this brutal treatment of Baker and his family. They never forgave Munro for attempting to kidnap Baker. As for Munro, he rushed to the New York governor with a bitter complaint. But it wasn't a complaint about Ethan or the Green Mountain Boys this time. It was a complaint about his own posse. Yorker posses seemed to lose their interest a bit too rapidly whenever it came to a showdown with the Bennington Mob.

Governor Tryon studied Munro's report. It was becoming more and more apparent that the average Yorker citizen could not be depended upon in the landlords' attempts to take feudalism into the Grants. It was obvious too that the general run of Yorker had a sneaking sympathy for men who were fighting for their homes, for the right to own the farms that they had hacked out of the wilderness.

Dolefully reviewing the situation, Governor Tryon slowly came to realize that only a superb regiment of British troops, armed to the teeth and with no sneaking sympathies for the settlers on the Grants, could ever defeat the Green Mountain Boys.

5

Kidnapers in Red Coats

Convinced that the struggle was hopeless, Governor Tryon decided to make a pretense of offering peace. Not only had he come to realize that he couldn't depend on his own armed forces, but he had recently been warned by the home government in England that he couldn't expect to call on the regulars for aid. The British, whatever their attitude was later on toward the Colonists, wanted the Grants properly settled. The quicker the Grants were occupied, the less chance there was of the French recapturing the land they had lost to the British. But the British weren't particularly interested in protecting the big Yorker landlords who were only eager to settle the land for their own profit.

Governor Tryon, therefore, held out the olive branch. He asked that the people of the Grants send him men from Bennington who could carry on negotiations. But he made it quite clear that he didn't care to deal with an outlaw like Ethan Allen.

The good people of Bennington eagerly dispatched two men who they thought would be acceptable. But no sooner had the emissaries arrived in New York than Ethan learned that Cockburn was back in the Grants running lines again. Cockburn was now a deputy of the surveyor general of New York. For a Yorker surveyor, and an official at that, to appear in the Grants when negotiations for peace were under way was like trying to come to terms with an angry bull while a red flag is waved under his nose. At the first rumor that Cockburn was back, Ethan raised the wolf call. Within a few hours, Baker, Seth Warner and a band of Green Mountain Boys had started north.

They caught Cockburn red-handed, smashed his compass, broke up his chain and rapidly escorted him and his linesmen out of the Grants. Then they descended upon a settlement of tenant farmers who had been placed in the vicinity by a Yorker landlord named Colonel Reid. The settlers had built themselves cabins and were blithely farming and operating a water-powered gristmill. The Boys, at the point of their guns, ran the settlers off the land.

Infuriated by this, which he considered a hostile act while peace terms were being discussed, Tryon broke off negotiations. Then he offered a reward of twenty pounds for Ethan's capture.

Twenty pounds was a large sum of money to pay for the capture of any man. But for the capture of Ethan who, besides being a dead shot was very handy with his fists, the price was none too attractive. Only the most foolhardy could have been willing to tackle the job.

However, there are always fools in the world and when a group of British regulars stationed at Crown Point learned that Ethan was in the vicinity, they decided their time had come to turn an honest penny. Through a spy they were informed that Ethan and a friend of his, Eli Robards, were lodging for the night in a nearby tavern run by a man named Richardson and his daughter.

Arming themselves with enough guns to capture a regiment, the squad of regulars walked in on Ethan while he was eating supper. If they hadn't been the fools they were, they would have nabbed Ethan then and there while his guard was down. But they made the mistake of pretending they hadn't recognized him.

Ethan, who was smart enough to realize instantly what they had come for, knew he was trapped. But he also knew that when one is trapped it is always wise to play for time and watch for an opening. Not for a moment losing his presence of mind, Ethan called for a bowl of punch in honor of these gallant soldiers of King George.

"Make it strong, landlord!" he shouted. "Spike it well with rum!"

When the bowl was brought and set on the table before the soldiers, Ethan offered a toast to the King. The soldiers drank with right good will. Their plan was coming off better than they had expected. Here was their simple-minded quarry, totally unaware of their purpose and buying them drinks into the bargain.

"A toast to General Gage!" Ethan shouted. "Drink hearty, men!"

More punch was drunk. Another bowl was ordered. Even Governor Tryon himself was toasted. The regulars slapped each other on the back and

The regulars laughed at the joke on Ethan.

roared with laughter at the joke on Ethan. It wasn't often that they could mix duty with pleasure. The woods around the Richardson place echoed with the merrymaking.

Finally Ethan rose to his feet. His prospective captors, pretty tipsy by this time, noticed with satisfaction that Ethan seemed more tipsy than they were. He positively staggered as he lurched into the kitchen to command another bowl. Moreover his friend Eli had collapsed completely and lay snoring with his head on the table. Soon both men would be helpless.

The soldiers winked drunkenly at one another and nodded toward Eli's and Ethan's guns leaning in a far corner of the taproom.

Ethan returned from the kitchen, followed by pretty Miss Richardson bringing another bowl of punch. Everyone toasted the blushing young lady. Songs were sung. Finally Ethan suggested that the regulars help him lug Eli out to the barn. There the two could bed down on a pile of hay and sleep off the punch.

"We'll leave our guns here," Ethan mumbled. "Mistress Richardson will take care of them for us."

With shouts and laughter the squad of soldiers carried Eli and helped Ethan, who seemed hardly able to walk, out to the barn. There they dropped the two into the hay. Leaving them snoring there, they tottered back to the taproom to celebrate the capture of the Hampshire men by finishing the rest of the punch.

Their celebration of the capture was a bit premature. As soon as the Britishers had tottered out of sight, Ethan and Eli sprang to their feet. They emptied their boots of the punch they had secretly poured into them and then circled back to the tavern. Pretty Miss Richardson, who had been taking care of their guns, hastily passed them out through an open window. In a moment Eli and Ethan were on their way through the woods bound for Shoreham.

Far behind them they could hear the drunken Britishers crashing through the brush, firing off their muskets and cursing their luck. Their brief merrymaking with Ethan and Eli had cost them plenty.

But it had been a close escape for Ethan and he

knew his life was in danger. So far as the province of New York was concerned, he was its principal target. For without any position that could be called official, he had become the accepted leader in the fight to protect the Grants from Yorker rule. And he was not only the Grants' military leader, he was the spokesman as well.

Ethan's pen was always ready to defend the settlers of the Grants in print. Newspapers in Connecticut and elsewhere published his articles in which the theme was always "Life, Liberty and Property." People read and re-read what he wrote. In those days newspapers were few and they were read with care and respect. Articles and news items printed in them were discussed at length at home and in public places.

The general store where people bought everything from molasses to hairpins was a sort of public forum, a place where a little town meeting was held every weekday. Every man was his own news

Ethan wrote articles on "Life, Liberty and Property."

commentator, but unlike present-day news commentators of radio and television each one could be answered back and argued with. Some of the arguments in the general store were likely to be pretty lively and often the fur would fly.

Ethan enjoyed a good argument. His articles about the struggle over the Grants started many hot arguments throughout New England. Most New Englanders took Ethan's side, for like him they believed in "Life, Liberty and Property." All but the rankest Tories felt a sort of kinship with the settlers in the Grants. They realized that the time might soon come when they, too, would have to take up arms and fight for their homes. The Green Mountain Boys, they realized, were already defending the Yankee way of life against that of old Europe.

While Ethan was busy writing his articles defending the rights of his fellow settlers, the Yorkers were laying new plans to invade the Grants. A Colonel Reid, whose tenants had been run off the land he claimed under a New York patent, decided to bring in a new batch of settlers. He managed to round up a large number of innocent immigrants who had just arrived in New York City from Scotland. The Colonel knew that they would have no prejudice against being tenant farmers. He knew too that they wouldn't realize he was in effect moving them onto an active volcano. The Colonel painted a bright picture of the peaceful life in the Grants. Among the friendly hills, he told them, they would feel very much at home.

The Scottish immigrants sailed up the Hudson and hopefully moved into the Grants with their wives and children. But they hadn't been able to build more than a dozen log cabins and erect a gristmill when news of their invasion was brought to Ethan. Gathering a hundred or so Green Mountain Boys, he started for their settlement.

Arrived there, the Boys found no one around except the womenfolk. And the Scottish lassies spoke with such a thick burr that the Boys couldn't understand a word the girls said. They gathered, however, that the Scotsmen were off somewhere cutting hay. Scouts soon found them and brought them back. Ethan briefly informed them that their landlord, Colonel Reid, had no rights to the land he had rented to them. If they wished to purchase land with a New Hampshire title they would be permitted to stay on. But not as Reid's tenants.

Then he ordered his Boys to burn down the cabins, pull down the gristmill, smash the big millstone and dump it over the falls. Before noon the little settlement lay in ashes and the bewildered Scottish settlers were trudging back toward New York.

One can't help sympathizing with these innocent Scots who had come into the Grants without being warned by their landlord that they might run into trouble. Some of them, it is true, remained and bought land from New Hampshire men. But Ethan was determined to keep out tenant farming, no matter who the tenants were. The right to own property was basic with Ethan and anyone who threatened that right was liable to get hurt.

News of this latest outrage soon reached Governor Tryon. Colonel Reid had drawn up the usual affidavits describing in hair-raising prose the Green Mountain Boys' destruction of his colony. Tryon angrily called his council together. The council deliberated. It had deliberated before and it deliberated again. This time it advised the Governor that the time had at last come to call upon the British general to occupy Fort Ticonderoga and Crown Point with British regulars. If the Green Mountain Boys started any more fireworks the British troops could march into the Grants and restore order.

However, the British general did not take kindly to the Governor's request. If the Governor couldn't take care of a few "lawless vagabonds," said the general, the dignity of his high office wasn't worth defending. It was up to his own constabulary to handle the disorders in the Grants. It was not the business of British regulars. They had enough to do elsewhere, what with all New England showing signs of restlessness.

The general's decision not to intervene was another victory for Ethan's tactics. So long as the Green Mountain Boys were regarded as a mob of a few "lawless vagabonds" the Grants would be safe from an invasion by British troops. But in order to keep up the appearance of being a mob, it must act like one. It must be able to assemble rapidly, strike like lightning and melt away like summer snow.

Satisfied that his tactics were proving successful, Ethan decided to make his defenses more secure. Having cleared out Reid's settlers, he began building a fort. It was twenty by thirty-two feet and the log walls were a foot thick. In the second story three dozen loopholes were cut to shoot through. The roof was constructed so that it could be thrown off in case an attacking force set it on fire, and the fort itself was built over a bubbling spring so a besieged force wouldn't be driven out by thirst.

Having built the fort, Ethan garrisoned it with a platoon of Green Mountain Boys and waited for the Yorkers or British regulars to come around and try to start trouble.

6

The Boys Raise a Roof

For a long time a town in the Grants which the Hampshire men called Clarendon, but which the Yorkers insisted upon calling Durham, had been a thorn in Ethan's flesh. The settlers there boasted of living under a New York title and loudly announced that they planned to continue doing so. The leader of these Durhamites who rejoiced in

83

being subjects of Governor Tryon was Benjamin Spencer. Besides being a judge he was also an agent for "Old Swivel-Eye" Duane who owned large tracts of land thereabouts.

We still can read the letters that Judge Spencer wrote to his boss, Governor Tryon. They do not speak in very flattering terms of Ethan and his Green Mountain Boys. The judge called them "black-guard fellows" and accused them of swaggering around double-armed to protect their leader. He also complained that they had threatened to burn down his house and roast anyone who attempted to uphold New York.

It is quite likely that the Green Mountain Boys were overbearing and full of bluster. They acted this way deliberately, as a part of their tactics, but woe betide any man who thought they were bluffing and tried to prove it.

Ethan with a large gang of Green Mountain Boys had already paid Durham a visit. Warned

84

that they were coming, Justice Spencer had found a pressing engagement elsewhere. At least he was not around when Ethan arrived. However, Ethan warned the inhabitants that if they and their officials persisted in their ways, they might expect another visit. The second visit, he mildly suggested, might be something hotter than a housewarming.

As soon as Ethan and his "black-guard fellows" had departed, Justice Spencer came out of the woods where he had been holding court with the squirrels. His courage restored by Ethan's departure, he bravely announced that he would continue issuing writs of ejectment against Hampshire men, come what may.

This sort of open defiance had never pleased Ethan. He may have been a loud talker, but his threats were not empty ones. There was always a hard core to everything Ethan said. That is one of the reasons the Boys stuck by him. If he had been a mere blowhard, he wouldn't have lasted ten minutes among a set of hard-fisted, hard-headed pioneers.

Back to Durham went Ethan with a company of more than a hundred Green Mountain Boys. This time they managed to catch Justice Spencer before he had time to find another pressing engagement elsewhere. A small group, led by Ethan, went to the Judge's house at eleven o'clock at night when he and his family were in bed.

According to Spencer's report of the episode, Ethan burst into his bedroom armed with a brace of pistols and his flintlock. He ordered the Judge out of bed and told him to waste no time in doing so. When the Judge seemed too slow about pulling on his breeches, Ethan, according to Spencer, hit him over the head with his gun. Other Green Mountain Boys stood outside the house poking their fowling pieces through the bedroom windows. Mrs. Spencer and the children stood screaming in the corner. Evidently they weren't of the same rugged material as 'Member Baker's wife and small son who had sailed into the fray when they saw the old man being mistreated by the Yorker kidnapers.

When the Judge finally got his breeches on (it was a cold night in late November) he was escorted to a nearby inn where the Boys held him prisoner. On the following morning he was visited by a man named Hough who claimed to be a parson but who was also a justice of the peace under a New York commission. He protested the treatment Ethan was giving Spencer and ordered Ethan and his Boys to clear out of Durham.

According to the report Parson Hough sent Tryon, Ethan's language was bloodcurdling. Ethan declared that "If ever they had to come to Durham again they would lay it in ashes and leave every person in it a corpse." He also announced that he meant to have Spencer tried on the following day

Ethan ordered the Judge out of bed.

and he asked the Judge where he wanted the trial to take place. Justice Spencer thought it over and then replied that he'd like to be tried on the front stoop of his own home.

Ethan pleasantly agreed to this and a day later the trial was held on Spencer's front steps. By that time more Green Mountain Boys had gathered to see the fun. They joined the citizens of Durham who were anxious to see Ethan and his men hold one of their famous "judgment seats."

To the cheers of the Boys and the wonderment of the Durhamites, Ethan, Seth Warner, Remember Baker and Robert Cochran, wearing their coonskin hats and their buckskin shirts, seated themselves on the bench in front of Spencer's house. Then they told the Judge to take off his hat and stand at attention while he heard the charges against him.

Ethan read the charges. Spencer, he said, was guilty of "cuddling with the land jobbers of New York," he was guilty of issuing writs of ejectment against Hampshire men, and of sending numerous complaints about the Green Mountain Boys to Governor Tryon. As the charges were self-evident, Spencer admitted them all and was found guilty. After deliberating for a few minutes, the judges announced that as punishment Spencer's house was to be burned down.

Spencer was aghast. He pointed out that burning down his house would be a hardship not so much on him as on his wife and children. The house contained all his worldly goods, his clothing, his furniture. His family would be left destitute if such a sentence were carried out.

The four men listened silently to Spencer's plea. They may have been hard as nails—history has given them that reputation—but evidently their justice was tempered with the milk of human kindness. Seth Warner spoke up. After consulting the other members of the "judgment seat," he was pleased to announce that the sentence would be a less harsh one. Instead of burning the house, the Green Mountain Boys would merely remove the roof.

"Remove the roof!" Judge Spencer was thunderstruck.

The four judges nodded. "The Boys will remove the roof," said Warner, "but they will also replace it. But on one condition."

"And what is that?" Judge Spencer stammered.

"That it goes back under a good New Hampshire title."

Judge Spencer immediately agreed. Standing before the four men, he gave silent thanks that he and his family had escaped more severe punishment.

Ethan stood up. He waved his hat toward the roof. "Take it off, boys," he said.

Full of high spirits, the Green Mountain Boys enthusiastically removed the roof of Judge Spencer's house. From the reports that have come down to us they did it "with great shouting and much noise and tumult." Then, just as enthusiastically, they put it back again, but this time under a good New Hampshire title—after Judge Spencer had bought the land from New Hampshire.

Other Durhamites, not wishing to see their roofs removed, followed suit and exchanged their New York titles for New Hampshire ones. But rumors soon reached Ethan in Bennington that a few greedy New Hampshire land-jobbers had raised their prices in Durham, hoping to make a profit on sales to the citizens there. Angered by the news, Ethan immediately wrote a letter to the Durhamites to reassure them. He notified them that his Green Mountain Boys were at any moment ready to assist them "in mobbing such avaricious persons" and that any greedy land-jobbers, no matter who they were, would get a dose of the twigs of the wilderness if they didn't behave. Remember Baker appended his signature to the letter, as did Seth Warner, who also offered his services to the Durhamites in case they needed an adviser.

This friendly gesture seems to have pacified the Durhamites, but it had just the opposite effect on the New York governor and his council. Another resolution was passed. It raised the reward for Ethan's capture to a hundred pounds and warned the leaders of the Bennington "mob" that if they didn't surrender to the New York authorities within seventy days they'd be hanged without trial.

Ethan and his men did not take this warning as

a joke. They vowed that if any New York sheriff should lay his hand on any one of them they'd shoot him down. To make their position clear, Ethan wrote one of his blistering letters. He told the Yorker officials that if "you insist upon killing us to take possession of our 'Vineyards', come on, we are ready for a game of scalping." Then he ordered his Green Mountain Boys to make ready for a wolf hunt.

Alarmed by this display of force, Justice Hough, still full of his own importance but still loyal to New York, threatened action. The Boys laughed at him. They told him that if he valued his health he had better resign his position as a Yorker official. They made it clear that they had no intention of seeing their leaders hanged.

Hough should have known that the Green Mountain Boys meant what they said. But he evidently believed that when an angry bull comes charging at you it isn't necessary to take to your heels. He believed a person should stand his ground

93

and quote Blackstone on the law of trespass.

Filled with indignation at the Green Mountain Boys' threat to shoot down any Yorker who dared arrest their leaders, Hough hustled off to tell Governor Colden. Colden had taken Tryon's place while the latter was in England trying to persuade the King to give him British troops to put down the rebellion in the Grants. Hough told his story to Colden, embellishing it with all sorts of horrible details. The Green Mountain Boys, he said, were dangerous rioters who didn't care a pin for law and order and had no respect for his official position as justice of the peace.

Having delivered himself of this message, Hough returned to Durham, still boiling with righteous indignation. It would have been better for him if he had stayed within shouting distance of the governor. As soon as he returned the Green Mountain Boys paid him a visit. Hough says that he knocked one of them down and then climbed onto a rock where he held them at bay by sheer force of character. But that is his own story.

At any rate, thirty armed men, led by Peleg Sunderland, captured Hough, tossed him into a sleigh and carried him to Sunderland some forty miles away. He was held there until Ethan Allen and Seth Warner could get up from Bennington to hold a seat of justice.

The seat of justice this time was a large one. There were seven judges on the bench and Hough was marched up before them, surrounded by men with drawn swords. He was charged with having complained to the Governor of New York about the treatment of Spencer, with having tried to persuade the citizens of Durham not to have dealings with the Green Mountain Boys, and with having acted in the Grants as a New York official. Hough admitted all the charges against him.

The seven judges then withdrew to a neighboring farmhouse. They were gone a long time. As there was no question of Hough's guilt they evidently spent the time deciding on the punishment. It is quite likely that Remember Baker and some of the fiery-tempered Boys would have hanged Hough, but Ethan Allen and Seth Warner always stood for moderation. The punishment they finally decided upon seems extreme today, though Hough probably considered himself lucky to have got off as easily as he did. The judges ordered that he be stripped to the waist and given two hundred lashes.

The sentence was immediately put into effect. Hough was tied to a tree and four men provided with rope ends administered the flogging, spelling one another when their arms tired.

It was cruel punishment and the best that can be said of it is that it was the last serious whipping administered in the Grants. Moreover, it had its effect. Hough cleared out of the Grants on the following morning, his injuries not being serious enough to keep him from traveling, and made his way post haste to New York City.

It was the last serious whipping administered in the Grants.

He at once petitioned the governor's council for an armed force to protect him from the Green Mountain Boys. The council thought it over. Their final decision was hardly what one would call thrilling. As a reward for their official's single-handed though pig-headed fight against the Green Mountain Boys, they granted him the right to beg for his living.

Hough never returned to the Grants, either to beg or to try to enforce order. He disappears from history at this point. But many other men and many incidents disappear at this point in the whirlpool of a greater conflict. Even the bitter struggle between the Grants and the province of New York was forgotten. For on April 19, 1775, a band of embattled farmers in Lexington fired the shot that was heard 'round the world.

7

Capture of the Fort

News that war with England had broken out into the open spread through the colonies as swiftly as horseflesh and shoe leather could carry it. The news wasn't unexpected. Everyone had known war was coming but no one was quite so ready for action as the Green Mountain Boys.

Not that the Boys could be called professional soldiers. The uniforms or, rather, the clothes they wore differed according to each man's taste. But in general they wore what every frontiersman wore at the time—a coat of fringed buckskin, linsey-woolsey shirts, homespun breeches and moccasins. They sported every variety of hat—coonskin, beaver, bear, squirrel, felt—in any shape a loving wife or sister fashioned it.

As for drilling or boot training, they wouldn't have known the difference between "Squads right!" and "About face!" They might have known what "Present arms!" meant, but the arms they presented would have made a British army officer laugh in their faces. There was not a bayonet among them!

But if the Green Mountain Boys weren't equipped with bayonets, their guns were dangerous in another way. For many of them carried rifles. And their rifles were deadly.

Every frontiersman who could afford one carried a rifle. It was a weapon generally unknown except in frontier territory like the Grants. Folks in the rest of New England carried muskets with a smooth bore. They were short, heavy, .75-calibre guns with a kick that would knock over a medium-sized horse. One didn't sight with a musket, one merely pointed it in the general direction of the target. And anybody who could hit a barn door at fifty paces deserved a sharpshooter's medal.

The rifles the Green Mountain Boys carried were different. As the name implies they weren't smooth-bore guns. Their barrels were rifled; that is to say, the inner core of the gun was grooved with a twist. This gave the bullet a spin. When a bullet travels with a spin it travels in a straighter line, it travels farther and its aim is ten times more accurate.

The kind of rifle used by Ethan Allen, Remember Baker, Seth Warner and many other Green Mountain Boys had been developed by immigrant German gunsmiths in Pennsylvania. It was a long, lank, beautiful gun and as accurate as a modern rifle up to 100 yards. Frontiersmen needed a light and highly accurate gun. They depended on their guns for food and some of their clothing.

Moreover, they had to travel light when they hunted and the bullets for their rifles weighed only half an ounce—much less than those for muskets.

The Green Mountain Boys, like their fellow frontiersmen in Kentucky and Virginia, were dead shots with their rifles. They had to be if they and their families wanted to eat during the winter. So they were expert hunters as well as expert marksmen. And now, when a shooting war had begun, they were dangerous men when they began sighting down their long rifle barrels from behind a tree at an enemy's red coat. Far beyond the range of a British musket, they could pick off the British like sitting ducks.

Ethan was proud of his sharpshooters. He knew how valuable they would be as soldiers in this new fight for liberty. As soon as the news of war with England reached him, he forgot his fight with the province of New York. "The first systematical and bloody attempt at Lexington to enslave America," he wrote, "thoroughly electrified my mind, and fully determined me to take part with my country." He at once issued a call for the Green Mountain Boys to assemble. Within less than a month after the Battle of Lexington, Ethan was ready for an attack on Fort Ticonderoga.

Fort Ticonderoga had been built by the French. It was designed by a famous French military architect named Vauban and had countless clever devices for repelling an attacking force. Its real importance, however, lay in the fact that it guarded the waterways formed by Lake Champlain, Lake George and the Hudson River. Placed on a promontory jutting out into Lake Champlain at its junction with Lake George, its guns could prevent any enemy ship from sailing past. In other words, it dominated the gateway from Canada. And as any communication had to be by water, the fort, if held by Americans, could prevent an attack from the north.

After the Peace of Paris, the fort came into the hands of the British. They had let it fall into disrepair, but its position alone gave the fort a high importance. Everyone in the Grants realized this, and they were not the only ones who did. Every patriot in New England knew that Fort Ticonderoga must be captured at the very outset of hostilities with England. However, it was a group of influential citizens of Hartford who were the first to come to Ethan's aid. Recognizing his need for money, they obtained three hundred pounds from the Colony's treasury and sent it on to Ethan to buy powder and pay his men.

With characteristic energy, Ethan had mustered all the Green Mountain Boys in the vicinity of Bennington. Then he dispatched a rider to bring down the Boys from the north. He set May 10th as the time for the attack and he needed as large a force as he could muster. The rendezvous was to take place at Hand's Cove on the shores of Lake Champlain.

A spy whom Ethan sent secretly to the fort had returned with an encouraging report. He had managed to get inside by posing as a bewhiskered frontiersman in search of the company barber. He got his shave, a close one according to his story, but he managed to pick up a good deal of general information from the barber.

The spy learned, among other details, that the garrison consisted only of about fifty British regulars—enough to keep one barber busy, but hardly enough to protect a large fortress like Ticonderoga. Moreover, the place was in a worse state of repair than it appeared from the outside.

Despite this encouraging report, Ethan knew that if the British ever got wind of the attack, fifty men on the alert could easily wipe out a much larger attacking force. If Fort Ticonderoga was to be captured, it must be done by a surprise assault.

All night long under a waning moon, the Green Mountain Boys from all sections of the Grants poured into Hand's Cove. They brought their own food and their own long rifles, but Ethan supplied the powder and bullets. Grouped in the shadows of the trees they stood leaning on their guns, chewing tobacco and waiting for Ethan to give them the word to move.

A short while after midnight the men were surprised to see an officer, clad in the brilliant scarlet coat of the Connecticut governor's foot guards, suddenly appear at the rendezvous. An attendant was with him. He had evidently ridden his horse hard for it stood steaming with sweat in the chill morning air. The officer loudly asked for the whereabouts of Mr. Allen. He had ridden all night, he said, and it was imperative for him to see the commander of the Green Mountain Boys at once.

Some of the Boys led him to the campfire where Ethan stood talking to a group of his officers. The stranger in his scarlet coat announced that he was Benedict Arnold. He also announced in a loud voice that the Committee of Safety in Cambridge, Massachusetts, had placed him in command of the attack on Fort Ticonderoga. Then he waved his commission under Ethan's nose and demanded that the command of the Green Mountain Boys be turned over to him.

Ethan quietly listened to Arnold's heated demands, but the Green Mountain Boys gathered around the flickering fire were startled. They stood staring at this officer in his flashy coat, but when he began demanding that Ethan step down they began to murmur. When they had enlisted, it had been agreed that they could select their own officers. Without a second thought they had chosen Ethan Allen and Seth Warner. And now who was this whippersnapper in a scarlet jacket demanding that he be placed in full command?

The Boys began speaking up. They had always been outspoken and now they were more outspoken than ever. They said that if they couldn't serve under Ethan as their commander they wouldn't serve at all. They'd sling their rifles over their shoulders and march back to the hills.

Benedict Arnold, who had evidently never encountered such outspoken and independent frontiersmen, was dumbfounded. It was his turn to stare at the uncouth-looking men with their home-made hats, their wicked looking rifles and their

Benedict Arnold demanded command.

self-confident airs. And what he saw made it plain
to him that he stood no chance at all of taking over
command.

Ethan, to avoid trouble from either Arnold or
his own men and to save the expedition from being
wrecked at the very start, offered to share command with Arnold, at least to permit him to trudge
along beside him at the head of the column. Ar-

nold accepted. Even if it meant little, it would look impressive from the sidelines.

That little matter settled, Ethan now had to tackle a new problem. The boats in which he had expected to ferry his troops across the lake hadn't arrived from Skenesboro. Unless he and his men could cross the lake under cover of darkness, there would be no chance of taking Ticonderoga by surprise.

Fortunately, however, just before dawn a large scow propelled by two boys and an old Negro who thought he was joining a wolf hunt crept up to the shore through the morning mist. It was followed by a smaller boat. By that time more than two hundred men had gathered for the attack, but the two boats, crowded to the gunwales, could hold only eighty-five. And it was now too close to sunrise for the boats to attempt a return trip.

Leaving Seth Warner to protect the rear, Ethan packed his men into the two boats. In a rising wind they started across the lake toward the fort. Ethan,

with Benedict Arnold behind him, stood in the
prow of the foremost boat, a sword in his hand.
Behind him the muffled oars churned the water
into drifting eddies of foam. The men, huddling
in the boats, talked in low voices.

After they had gone a mile across the water the
gray walls of the fort loomed through the mists
above them. The boats nudged up to the shore and
Ethan jumped nimbly to land. Arnold followed.
In a low voice Ethan ordered his men to line up.
He delivered a brief talk.

"Friends and fellow soldiers," he said, "you
have for a number of years past been a scourge and
terror to arbitrary power. . . . I now propose to
advance before you and, in person, conduct you
through the wicket gate; for we must this morning either quit our pretensions to valor, or possess
ourselves of this fortress in a few minutes; and as
it is a desperate attempt which none but the brav-
est men dare undertake, I do not urge it on any
contrary to his will. You who will undertake vol-
untarily, poise your firelocks."

Every man raised his gun.

At Ethan's command the Boys started climbing the rocky hill toward the fort. Ethan and Benedict Arnold headed the column, their swords gleaming in the half-light of dawn. Across the lake the first glimmering of morning showed in the eastern sky beyond the sleeping hills of the Grants. A waning moon, pale like a ghost, hung in the west above the fort. In the stillness the wild cry of a loon drifted across the lake. Ethan climbed stealthily toward the wicket gate.

Would the surprise attack succeed? Or had the British garrison received warning of the attack?

The question was soon answered. A sentry, an hour glass running low beside him, lay sprawled in deep slumber on a bench by the wicket gate. His snores rasped through the chill morning air. Evidently the garrison in the barracks was soundly sleeping too.

Suddenly the guard, yanked into wakefulness by the sound of a broken twig, leaped to his feet. In an instant he had his musket to his shoulder. He

Dropping his musket, the guard at Fort Ticonderoga took to his

heels. Behind him stormed Ethan and the Green Mountain Boys.

aimed point-blank at Ethan, pulled the trigger. There was a flash. But it was only the flash of powder in the pan. The gun had misfired.

Dropping his musket, the guard took to his heels, bellowing a warning. Ethan gave chase. Behind him stormed the Green Mountain Boys brandishing their rifles and uttering war whoops. They swarmed through the gate, yelling "No quarter!" Reaching the barracks, they began pounding on the doors with their guns.

A British regular opened the door. He was armed and made a lunge at one of the Boys with his bayonet. Quick as a flash Ethan floored him with the flat of his sword. Believing that Ethan meant to run him through, the man yelled for mercy. Ethan spared his life, but on condition that he would lead him to the commandant's quarters. Shaking with terror, the Britisher took Ethan to an outside stairway leading up one flight to a door in the west barracks.

Followed by Benedict Arnold and a crowd of Boys, Ethan clattered up the stairs. A young British lieutenant, evidently awakened by the racket, peered out the door and then hastily withdrew, slamming the door behind him. Ethan banged on the door with the hilt of his sword.

"Come out of there!" he bawled.

A moment later the door swung open and Captain Delaplace, commandant of the fort, appeared. He hadn't had time to dress and he stood holding a sword in one hand and his red breeches in the other. He stared at Ethan and then glanced down at the milling crowd below. His face flushed with anger. He glowered at Ethan who stood before him with his sword.

"By whose authority," he demanded, "have you and your mob entered His Majesty's fort?"

Ethan's instant reply has passed into history. It is a remark that rings like the Liberty Bell itself— triumphant, vibrating, fearless.

"In whose name do I come here?" Ethan bellowed. "In the name of the Great Jehovah and the Continental Congress!"

The Boys cheered. Ethan, holding his sword over the commandant's head, demanded immediate and complete surrender. His Boys were to have possession of the fort, he said, "and all the effects of George the Third." Then he added that if this demand were not complied with, or if a single gun were discharged at any of his men, "neither man, woman or child should be left alive."

Realizing that it was hopeless to resist, Captain Delaplace handed Ethan his sword and gave orders to his men to turn out and parade before Ethan without their arms.

The Captain's orders were unnecessary. His bewildered soldiers had already been routed out of their bunks by the Green Mountain Boys. They now stood shivering in their nightshirts, wondering what had happened. Ethan ordered his men to line up the prisoners. After their guns had been collected, they were ordered back to their quarters where they were placed under guard.

Meanwhile Seth Warner's men had begun to arrive, having ferried themselves across from Hand's Cove. Fort Ticonderoga having already been captured, Ethan ordered Seth Warner and his men to capture Crown Point, fifteen miles down the lake.

It had taken scarcely an hour to capture the fort, and it had been done without any loss of life. It was another bloodless triumph for Ethan. To celebrate the victory, he opened up the Captain's wine cellar. Rum was handed around "for the refreshment of the fatigued soldiery," as Ethan explained, and a celebration began.

Benedict Arnold, unaccustomed to the high spirits and wild ways of the Green Mountain Boys, tried to put a damper on the merrymaking. But to little purpose. At the height of the festivities, according to Arnold's own diary, several of the Boys expressed their joy over the victory by taking a few pot shots at him. From the very start they had taken an instinctive dislike to this smartly dressed officer who was later to betray his country.

But not all the firing of guns was directed at Arnold. Matthew Lyon, an enthusiastic Irishman, discovered a thirteen-inch mortar familiarly known as "Old Sow." There was plenty of powder in the fort's magazine and Lyon helped himself to a bucketful. He filled "Old Sow" to the muzzle and fired off a blast that could have been heard in Canada. Folks across the lake in the Grants were soon aware that the fort had fallen to Ethan. They began celebrating too.

But they weren't the only ones. The whole country went wild with delight over the victory. As soon as the fort had been captured, Ethan had dispatched couriers posthaste bearing the news of this first triumph over the British.

"I make you a present," he wrote to Governor Trumbull of Connecticut, "of a major, a captain and two lieutenants in the regular establishment of George the Third. I hope they may serve as ransom for some of our friends in Boston."

Then he sent a rider bearing the fort's flag to Philadelphia. There it was to be presented to the Continental Congress in whose name, along with that of the Great Jehovah, Ethan had captured it.

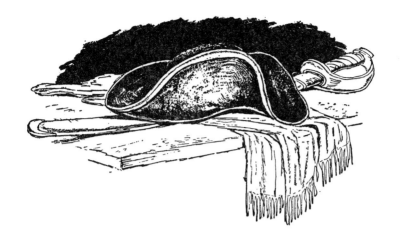

8

The Dark Days Begin

The capture of Fort Ticonderoga was the high point of Ethan's career. From then on his life was beset by misfortune and plagued by the snubs of his fellow countrymen.

To begin with, the Continental Congress did not receive news of Ethan's brilliant victory with any great enthusiasm. Though it had stirred the country to general rejoicing, the members of the Congress took a dim view of it. The gift of the fort with all its valuable cannon and military supplies embarrassed them. They felt it inadvisable at the time to advertise to the world that the Colonies had taken the offensive against England.

Ethan was therefore stunned when a letter arrived from Congress ordering that the cannon and military stores captured at Ticonderoga be removed to the south end of Lake George. They were to be held there, Congress said, so that they might be safely returned to His Majesty George the Third when the "former harmony" between America and England "so ardently wished for" by the Colonies could be restored.

Boiling mad, Ethan reached for his pen. He wrote a long letter to Congress protesting against the removal of the guns from the fort. He pointed out that it would leave the entire northern area wide open to attack by the British.

What was more, he wished to take advantage of the victory. He believed in striking again and striking quickly. He urged Congress to "push the war against the King's troops in Canada" and suggested that Montreal be captured. He estimated that from two to three thousand men could do it. "Advancing an army into Canada," he wrote, "will be agreeable to our friends; and it is bad policy to fear the resentment of an enemy."

Soon after Ethan had sent off the letter, he called a council of officers to discuss a Canadian campaign. Seth Warner was present along with Remember Baker, Major Samuel Elmore of the Connecticut forces and several others. The council decided to send Ethan and Warner to Philadelphia to argue for the campaign. Then all present signed a petition to Congress, praising Ethan's courage and initiative in taking Fort Ticonderoga.

The next morning Ethan and Warner started for Philadelphia. On the way Ethan stopped off at Bennington to attend church. There is a famous story that during the service Parson Jedediah Dewey offered up a prayer for the successful capture of the fort, thanking the Great Jehovah for His assistance. Fidgeting in his pew, Ethan finally interrupted the minister by bawling out, "Parson

Dewey! Parson Dewey! Don't forget that I was there!" To which the good parson is supposed to have replied, without raising his eyes, "Sit down, Ethan Allen. When I want you I will call upon you." And continued praying.

Aside from the fact that Ethan was probably not so unmannerly as to have bawled out something during church service, it is doubtful if Parson Dewey would have answered him. The story probably has no foundation in fact.

On June 23, 1775, Seth Warner and Ethan Allen appeared before the Continental Congress. As Ethan looked around Carpenter's Hall at the seated delegates he could see a number of his old enemies. "Old Swivel-Eye" Duane was there with some of his Yorker friends. They stared sourly at Ethan and Warner, but evidently the two heroes from the Grants made a good impression on the other delegates. They voted to pay off the Green Mountain Boys and their officers who had captured Fort Ticonderoga. But what was even more satisfying to Ethan, they authorized the organization of a regiment of Boys under such officers as they themselves should choose.

Full of high hopes, Ethan hurried back to Bennington. He at once started enlisting recruits. There was no doubt in his mind that he would be given command of a regiment of Green Mountain Boys and he pictured himself at their head storming the walls of Montreal. But he was due for a savage blow to his pride.

Even though he had spearheaded the drive to keep the Yorkers out, even though he had planned the campaign against Ticonderoga and captured it, even though he had achieved both these victories without the loss of a single man, the people of the Grants refused to give Ethan Allen full honor. For when it came time to elect officers to command the Green Mountain Boys, the older men took over and Ethan was refused a commission. Seth Warner was chosen lieutenant colonel. Ethan's two brothers, Ira and Heman, were made officers. But Ethan himself was given no such honor.

It is difficult to explain why this should have happened. Ethan was deeply hurt by the rebuff and hardly understood the reason for it. There was one consolation left to him. It wasn't the young people who had demoted him. It was the cautious older folks who had put Seth Warner in command. They were afraid, perhaps, of Ethan's energy, imagination and high spirits. On the other hand, some historians say these older folks opposed Ethan because he was a land-jobber.

Even today this charge of land-jobbing is sometimes brought against Ethan. Some people insist that Ethan's main interest in life was protecting the property he owned. They even go so far as to say that his reason for capturing Fort Ticonderoga was to protect the Onion River Land Company of which he was part owner. But one might as well say that Benjamin Franklin and Robert Morris, no better patriots than Ethan, supported the Revolution because they had speculated in land and wished to protect it. Nearly everyone speculated in wild land in those days and Ethan was only one of many who did so.

As for the Onion River Land Company, it was begun on a shoestring and ended in bankruptcy. It never made much money for Ethan, his three brothers and Remember Baker, who were its only owners. Though at one time the company is said to have held more than 70,000 acres, much of this land was worth only a few pennies an acre. Compared to the big land companies of the time—the Holland Land Company with more than two and a half million acres, or the Ohio Company with a million and a half—the Onion River Company was a small business venture.

If any member of the Allen family was interested in making money it was Ira. He was the moving spirit of the Onion River Company, but his name is rarely listed among the moving spirits of the Green Mountain Boys. There is no doubt that Ira was interested in grabbing wild land to sell, and he ransacked the Grants looking for it. Sometimes Ethan went along with him. But we have it on the evidence of Ira's own autobiogra-

Ethan, refused a commission, was deeply hurt.

phy that his brother Ethan did not share his own passion for making money. During one of these prospecting trips Ira constantly accused Ethan of not attending to business. Instead of keeping his eye peeled for a good "pitch" of land, Ira sourly complained, Ethan always seemed more interested in bagging a twelve-point buck.

So it is hard to believe that all Ethan's activities were directed toward protecting his interests as a landowner. Yet this charge has so often been made that one cannot ignore it. Perhaps, though, one should look to the Green Mountain Boys themselves for a true evaluation of Ethan's character. Like all good frontiersmen, their sharp eyes would have been quick to detect any streak of greed or selfishness in their leader. Hadn't their keen glance seen through Benedict Arnold at the first encounter? As for Ethan, they had trusted him from the start. And though they recognized his failings, and he had many, they knew that these failings didn't include greed or hypocrisy. Left to themselves they would have followed him anywhere, but now when the time came they were not given the chance to elect him as their leader.

Cut to the quick by the Hampshire men's refusal to grant him a commission, Ethan let out some of his anger in a free-swinging row with Warner. But after that he took the snub like a good soldier. The Boys, however, who had followed him loyally, resented the snub. For a while it looked as if it might be impossible to raise recruits. However, when General Schuyler, who had been appointed by Congress to organize the attack on Montreal, arrived at Ticonderoga to take charge, Ethan swallowed his pride and offered his services without a rating.

Schuyler gave Ethan the dangerous job of going up to Canada and recruiting soldiers among the French settlers there. He did not succeed in getting many—under a hundred in all. Counting the thirty or so Americans with him, he now had a force of 110 men under his command. With his usual optimism Ethan believed that with this small force, aided by one under the command of a Massachusetts officer named John Brown, he could cross the St. Lawrence River and capture Montreal.

The plan misfired. Under cover of darkness Ethan ferried his troops across the river in canoes, a few at a time. But Brown and his men never showed up at the rendezvous. Whose fault this was will never be learned. Brown was killed soon after and as a result his side of the story has not come down to us.

However, it must be admitted that it was an ill-advised and ill-planned campaign. When an armed force of many hundreds of men from Montreal came down and attacked him, Ethan was trapped. His Canadian force melted away and with his back to the river Ethan was left fighting with only thirty-eight men, seven of whom were wounded. To prevent a general massacre, Ethan surrendered to the British officer leading the attack.

As he was about to hand over his sword, Ethan

was almost massacred himself. An enormous Indian, four paces away from where Ethan stood, raised his gun and aimed it point-blank at the Vermonter's heart. Quick as a flash Ethan seized the British officer by the shoulders and thrust him into the line of fire. Hardly had he done so when another Indian took aim. Ethan spun the officer around and, thus keeping the British officer between him and the two murderous Indians, prevented them from firing until an Irishman ran both off at the point of the bayonet.

Having thus escaped death, Ethan was then marched to Montreal, the British officer on one side and a French nobleman on the other. The Frenchman's eyebrow had been shot off during the brief fighting but he made merry over its loss. Ethan was treated courteously by his two captors, but it was a different story when he reached Montreal. He was brought before General Prescott, British commander at Montreal.

The General, who was obviously a fire-eater of the old school, asked Ethan his name. When

General Prescott threatened Ethan with his cane.

he learned that it was Ethan Allen he immediately inquired if this was the same Colonel Ethan Allen who had taken Fort Ticonderoga.

"I am that very man," Ethan replied.

Upon hearing this, General Prescott fell into a towering rage. His face grew crimson and he began threatening Ethan with his cane, meanwhile denouncing him as a traitor and a rebel.

Ethan stood his ground. He told the irate General that he was not accustomed to being caned by a Britisher and that he would knock the General down if he tried to do it. At this point a frightened English officer intervened. Plucking cautiously at the General's sleeve, he managed to whisper in his ear that caning a prisoner of war was beneath his dignity as a British officer and that he should calm down a bit.

The General took his officer's advice, but now he vented his fury on thirteen Canadian prisoners who stood before him. He loudly ordered a sergeant to bring up a squad of soldiers and bayonet the helpless captives on the spot.

The thought of such butchery was too much for Ethan. He pushed his way between the prisoners and their executioners, ripped open his shirt and asked that he be killed instead. The prisoners' only crime, he said, was loyalty to him. This act on Ethan's part, even though it reads like something in amateur theatricals, saved the lives of the prisoners.

However, it didn't help Ethan. General Prescott turned on him again in fury.

"I will not execute you now," he roared, "but you shall grace a halter at Tyburn!" referring to the gallows where many hapless creatures had been hanged.

Then he ordered the sergeant to hustle Ethan aboard the *Gaspee,* a British man-of-war then at anchor in the St. Lawrence River. This was immediately done. Aboard the ship, Ethan was dragged down into the darkness of the hold. Handcuffs were locked on his wrists while the ship's blacksmith attached heavy leg irons weighing thirty pounds to his ankles. There he was left.

It was the beginning of the blackest period in Ethan's life.

9

Ethan in British Irons

For six long weeks Ethan lay in the hold of the
Gaspee. The heavy leg irons made it impossible
for him to lie in any position other than on his
back. To relieve himself of some of the weight,
Ethan persuaded one of the guards to bring him
blocks of wood on which he could rest his leg
irons while he slept.

Somewhere old Dr. Samuel Johnson has said

that a ship is a floating prison. But what is a prison aboard a floating ship? Lying in painfully cramped quarters and in darkness, half starved, Ethan's life in the ship's hold became almost unbearable. To add to his misery the crew and the ship's officers, regarding him as an American rebel, took delight in abusing him. Among these tormentors was the ship's surgeon, a Dr. Dace, who passed his spare time bullying Ethan while he lay helpless in irons.

"You outlaw!" he would jeer. "You're ripe for the halter. Your rotting carcass has deserved death for years!"

One afternoon the doctor, egged on by the guards, had given Ethan a more merciless goading than usual. He knew that Ethan had a hot temper and he did his best to whip him into a fury. That afternoon the doctor succeeded, but he got more than he asked for. No longer able to withstand the jibes and insults, Ethan suddenly seized between his teeth the bent spike that held his irons, tore it free from its socket and, leaping to his feet, went after his tormentor. The doctor fled screaming with Ethan in hot pursuit. It was only with great difficulty that a half dozen guards could restrain the prisoner. When the irons were again adjusted, a padlock was employed instead of a bent spike.

"Blast your eyes!" one of the guards exclaimed, as he held Ethan. "Can you eat iron?"

After six weeks of this abusive treatment, Ethan and thirty-three other American prisoners were loaded onto a ship sailing for England. They were locked in a wooden cage built in the ship's hold. The trip to England took forty days. During this time none of the prisoners saw the light of day. Covered with filth and vermin, they were given no water to wash in and little water to drink. Many of the prisoners came down with dysentery.

That the men survived the ordeal—the misery, the hunger, the seasickness, the stench, the taunts of the crew, the lice, the darkness, the confinement—is a tribute to their strong hearts and bodies. For when the ship sailed into the harbor at Falmouth six weeks later, no man among the prisoners had died. But fearful suffering leaves a mark on any man and Ethan bore signs of his ill treatment for the rest of his life.

News that a batch of American prisoners had just arrived brought forth all the citizens of Falmouth to see them. A wild and bearded group they must have looked as they stumbled along the cobbled streets! Ethan, towering like a giant among his fellows, led the procession. He wore a red stocking-cap, a fawn-skin jacket fringed and double-breasted, breeches of serge and worsted stockings. People thronged the housetops to see the prisoners march by. At the gate of Pendennis Castle where the Americans were being taken, the crowd became so great that guards with drawn swords had to force a passage.

It was morbid curiosity that attracted the onlookers, for both they and the prisoners them-

Ethan towered like a giant among his fellow prisoners.

selves expected that there would soon be a mass hanging. Bets were already being placed in London that the prisoners would be hanged after a brief trial.

Still in handcuffs, the prisoners were locked up in the castle. Ethan, for all his sufferings, had not lost his old powers of persuasion. Somehow he managed to get permission to write Congress, and in his letter he described how the imprisoned Americans were being treated. He wrote that they were being dealt with not as prisoners of war but as criminals. Yet their life in prison was less bitter than their life had been on shipboard. They were allowed a breath of fresh air and a daily walk in the courtyard. People flocked to see them.

News of the arrival of a wild man from America who was as tall as Goliath and twice as terrifying to see had spread through the countryside. On Sunday afternoons folk came from miles around, bringing their wives, children or best girls to see Ethan. The jailers collected fees for ad-

mission and allowed the wandering yokels to talk
to the huge prisoner or even to feed him, much
as they might feed an elephant or a trained seal.
One English gentleman had his servant bring
Ethan a large bowl of punch. Ethan, to the aston-
ished delight of the spectators, drank it off in
one draught. Sometimes he made speeches. These
were not the kind that pleased his audience, for
their gist was that the British could never defeat
the Colonies. But Ethan delivered them mainly to
keep up his men's spirits. And his own.

After keeping Ethan and the others for two
weeks in Pendennis Castle, the British decided to
send the prisoners back to America. They were
again herded aboard a ship. Here Ethan's handcuffs, which he had worn night and day for fifteen weeks, were at last removed. But he and
the other prisoners were ordered below decks to
find what quarters they could in the black hole
where the anchor chain was stored. Ethan, for
all his courage and stout heart, later confessed

that at this point he gave way to complete despair. He became convinced that since the British government did not dare hang him, it meant to destroy him by neglect and hunger.

When good spirits fail, good health fails with them. Ethan believed that he would not live to see the green hills of Bennington again. Like all prisoners, he began to believe that he was forgotten by his friends and family, neglected by the government in whose behalf he had been taken captive. But in this moment of blackest despair there occurred one of those acts of charity that restored his belief in the basic goodness of human beings.

The man-of-war *Solebay* on which Ethan and his fellow prisoners were held dropped anchor on its way to America in the harbor of Cork, Ireland. There some Irishmen learned that Ethan and his men were aboard ship and were being miserably treated by the British.

In deep sympathy with the American Colonies for their rebellion against British rule, the warm-hearted Irishmen at once decided it was their duty to aid any American needing help. They raised a large sum of money to purchase supplies. When the captain of the *Solebay* had gone ashore, they rowed out to the ship with a cargo of presents.

A young officer in command of the ship during the captain's absence allowed the generous Irishmen to come aboard with their gifts. The gentlemen from Cork had not stinted themselves. To the ragged and hungry Americans they must have seemed like angels. To each of the thirty-four prisoners they brought a complete outfit of clothes, with an extra shirt and an overcoat. They presented them also with two pounds of tea and six pounds of brown sugar.

For Ethan their gifts were lordly indeed. They brought him a fine suit of clothes and enough superfine broadcloth to make himself two other suits. They brought him eight Holland linen shirts, silk and worsted hose, two pairs of shoes and two beaver hats, one of them richly laced with gold. They also presented him with a round of pickled beef, a number of fat turkeys, tea, chocolate, sugar in abundance, and bottled spirits to quench his thirst.

"We want to see you as well supplied with sea stores as the British captain himself," they told Ethan.

Nor was that all. A Mr. Hays of Cork presented Ethan with a finely embossed dagger and fifty pounds in gold. But Ethan kept only seven pounds of this sum for fear that the generous Irishmen might think him greedy.

From that day on Ethan had a soft spot in his heart for every Irishman he met. As well he might!

However, the story has an unhappy ending. When the captain of the *Solebay* returned to his ship and learned of the generosity of the gallant citizens of Cork, he flew into a rage. He vowed that "the American rebels should not be feasted at this rate by the rebels of Ireland." He took away most of Ethan's liquor and food and relieved the other prisoners of their tea and sugar. And when on the following day another boat

loaded down with gifts from some generous Dub-
liners arrived, the irate captain ordered it away.

On February 12, 1776, a fleet of forty-five
British ships, of which the *Solebay* was one, spread
its sails and set forth for America. It was carrying
an expedition under Lord Cornwallis to invade
North and South Carolina. Feeling against the
Yankee rebels ran high aboard the *Solebay*. Ethan
and his fellow prisoners soon learned that an army
transport, loaded with soldiers who are on their
way to kill one's fellow countrymen, is not the
place to find peace and comfort.

Not until May 8th, three long months after he
had left England, did Ethan see the distant shores
of his homeland. He was transferred to another
ship and taken up the coast to New York. Here
the ship dropped anchor off Sandy Hook. Two
of Ethan's Yorker friends—Governor Tryon and
Attorney General Kempe—both full-fledged
Tories by now—came aboard. They saw Ethan
as they stood chatting with the ship's officers, but
they only stared coldly at his withered frame, his

The prisoners began coming down with scurvy.

haggard face. Nevertheless, they had evidently recognized their old enemy from the Bennington hills, for after they had returned to the British ship on which they had taken refuge, the treatment accorded Ethan became worse than before.

During the long voyage across the wintry Atlantic, many of the prisoners had come down with scurvy. We know now that this disease is caused by lack of fresh fruit and vegetables, the lack of vitamins. But in those days men on ships perished of the disease without knowing how simply it could be cured. Ethan himself got a touch of it. But when he asked permission to buy food and medicine from the ship's store he was abruptly refused.

"You'll be hanged as soon as we can get you to Halifax," the captain told him. "Why should I make life easy for you rebels?"

Then, to emphasize his statement, the captain ordered the ship's doctor to refuse to treat any of the sick prisoners.

Perhaps it was the lack of medical care that saved the Yankee prisoners' lives. Certainly the treatment the British doctors administered seems rather primitive. When the ship reached Halifax the members of the crew suffering from scurvy were taken ashore at the doctor's orders and buried up to the neck in loose soil.

The Yankees, however, had somehow guessed what the real cure might be. One of them, dying of scurvy, bought with his last few pennies a basket of strawberries some friendly Indians had brought alongside the ship in their canoe. The Yankee ate them ravenously and, to the surprise of everyone, soon recovered. But when Ethan tried to procure more berries for the other sick men, he was unable to do so. Nevertheless, with the last remaining money the gentleman from Cork had given him, Ethan managed to buy a sack of onions which he and his fellow sufferers ate raw. Even in medicine, Ethan was in advance of his times.

It was now past the middle of October. Suddenly on October 20th orders were received to load the Americans onto a British frigate bound for New York. Again the miserable prisoners were herded aboard another ship. Except for the few weeks they had spent lodged in Pendennis Castle, Ethan's comrades had lain in the dark, stench-ridden, vermin-infested holds of enemy ships for more than a year.

Though Ethan expected further misery when he crawled weakly aboard the warship, he was due for a surprise. The captain had arranged a berth for the prisoners between decks and he invited Ethan to eat with him at his table. Accustomed only to the harshest treatment at the hands of the British skippers, Ethan was so touched by the offer that he burst into tears and could barely eat the food that was served him.

But his imprisonment aboard a ship was drawing to a close. During his voyages, New York City had been captured by the British and soon after the frigate reached there Ethan was put ashore. Now accorded the status of a captured officer, he was admitted to parole. This gave him freedom to move about the city, though his fellow prisoners, being privates, were locked up in the churches which the British were using as guardhouses.

Paroled in New York, Ethan managed to regain some of his health and high spirits. But his high spirits led him to break parole and he spent the next eight months in jail. On May 6, 1778, two years and seven months after his capture at Montreal, he was exchanged for a captured British officer. He was now free to return to the Grants where the Green Mountain Boys were still celebrating the great victory at Bennington. But before hurrying back home, Ethan traveled to Valley Forge to be greeted by General Washington. Although he was haggard from his long imprisonment, Ethan jauntily wore the beaver hat the gentlemen of Cork had presented him.

Washington introduced the big man from the Green Mountains to his staff of officers. Then he paid tribute to Ethan in a letter to Congress.

"I have been happy," Washington wrote, "in the exchange, and a visit from Lieutenant Colonel Allen. His fortitude and firmness seem to have placed him out of the reach of misfortune. There is an original something in him that commands admiration; and his long captivity and sufferings have only served to increase if possible, his enthusiastic zeal."

Washington, at least, appreciated Ethan's worth.

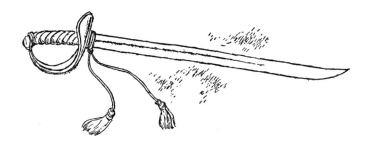

10

Back on the Warpath

Ethan arrived in Bennington on the evening of the last day of May, and the Green Mountain Boys greeted him with open arms. Many of his old friends had believed him dead. Now everyone rejoiced. Cannon were dragged forth onto the village green and fourteen salvos were fired—thirteen for the original states and one extra for young

Vermont. Though the Grants still had no statehood, it had a name now and a constitution.

Everyone gathered at the Catamount Tavern to hail the returned hero—the leader of the Green Mountain Boys who had captured Fort Ticonderoga, driven the Yorkers out of the Grants, been a martyr at Montreal, lain for long months as a prisoner on British ships, been starved, humiliated and abused. Now after two and a half years he was back home among his green hills and the people he loved.

Many times that night at the Catamount the punch bowl was filled. Countless toasts were drunk. Songs floated through the open windows of the tavern into the spring air. Ethan, still haggard and weak from ill treatment, delivered speeches and shook hands with all his friends and fellow citizens.

How glad they were that Ethan was safely back among them! But it wasn't only that. They needed him. The war was dragging and things didn't look

Everybody gathered at the Catamount Tavern to hail Ethan.

too hopeful for Washington's army. Canada had been lost, Fort Ticonderoga recaptured. British ships-of-war cruised ominously up and down Lake Champlain. Vermont was wide open to attack.

What is more, political enemies in Congress had refused to admit Vermont as a state. They were afraid New England might attempt to run the government and they did not wish to see another New England state added to the others. However, Vermont had a constitution. It was modeled after Pennsylvania's and recommended to the Vermonters by Ethan's old friend and tutor, Dr. Young. It was a fine constitution, one of the best in the country and the first to declare slavery illegal. Vermont was proud of it. But now Vermont needed a man who would defend her and fight for her rights.

No one had been able to take Ethan's place. Remember Baker had been killed, shot by an Indian from ambush in the first months of the war. Ethan's brother, Heman, had died from a cold contracted at the Battle of Bennington. Only Seth Warner could have filled Ethan's shoes, but even though he was a more able military man, Seth didn't have Ethan's fire.

It is true that Warner had led the Green Mountain Boys in the great victory at Bennington. Back in the taproom of the Catamount Ethan listened to the story of the battle from some of the Boys who had taken part in the fighting. It was still fresh in every Vermonter's mind for it had taken place that previous summer.

For some time General Burgoyne had been eyeing Bennington. He had heard that there were plenty of horses in that area and he needed mounts for his German dragoons. They had been clumping about in their enormous jack boots and leather breeches with no horses to ride and they had begun to complain. Burgoyne, encamped at Fort Edward, decided to find horses for them in Bennington.

For some reason he placed a German officer, who could speak no word of English, in command of the expedition. Most of the troops were professional soldiers, but there was a large contingent of Indians. The German general, whose name was Baum, started for Bennington. His dragoons plodded along in perfect discipline, but Baum soon realized that he had made a mistake in taking along the Indians. The undisciplined red men ranged ahead of the main body of troops. They looted

farms and shot down cattle in order to get the cowbells. Delighted with the sound, they danced ahead
of the troops, lustily ringing the cowbells. But this
warned the farmers ahead, who hastily drove off
their cattle and horses instead of leaving them
where Baum could pick them up.

In spite of the Indians, Baum and his troops
managed to reach a hill overlooking the Wallum-
scaik River just a few miles south of Bennington.
They dug themselves in and waited there for an
attack.

It soon came. General Stark, in command of
1500 New Hampshire men, and Seth Warner with
his 400 Green Mountain Boys had drawn up their
plan. Their men were to surround the hill, close
off the rear to a retreat and then make a frontal
attack.

At noon on August 16th the plan was put into
action and was an even greater success than had
been hoped for. Sticking paper in their hats so
Baum's men would think they were Tories, the

Yankees managed to creep up almost to the ene-my's lines. Then when the shooting started they fought Indian fashion, firing from behind trees while the Germans stood in close formation tak-ing the punishment like herded cattle. Meanwhile the Indians themselves, still jangling their cowbells, had escaped through the woods.

Burgoyne had sent Baum reinforcements but they were mighty slow in coming. They were German troops and they marched in rigid forma-tion, dressing their ranks every ten minutes and making only half a mile an hour marching time. Unfortunately they didn't arrive until the battle was almost over. Baum had been killed, the powder wagon blown up, and the dragoons who hadn't been killed were in full retreat.

It was at this point that Seth Warner and his Green Mountain Boys entered the fray. It was their job to meet the German reinforcements and wipe them out. They went about their task with zest. With their long rifles and their deadly aim, they soon had the reinforcements in full retreat. If darkness hadn't fallen Burgoyne's German reinforcements would have been completely annihilated.

The Battle of Bennington was one of the great victories of the Revolution. Two hundred Germans were killed and 700 captured, but the Americans lost only thirty killed and forty wounded. Moreover it was the turning point in the war with England, for it smoothed the way for the great victory at Saratoga a month later.

Ethan was proud of what Seth Warner and his Green Mountain Boys had done. He was sorry that he had not been there to help. But he was not back in Vermont for very long before he was leading them again in the old battle with Yorkers and Tories.

Groups of Yorkers and Tories had formed in Putney, Brattleboro and other towns north of Bennington for the purpose, as they said, "of opposing the pretended state of Vermont." They had drawn up resolutions which they had forwarded to Governor Clinton of New York, urging him to send troops to put down the "riotous men" who were trying to make Vermont a state. Clinton, not having learned Tryon's lesson, promised to squelch Ethan and his Green Mountain Boys once and for all.

This threat to his Boys was more than Ethan could stand. Legend tells us that Ethan jumped on his horse and rode out of Arlington with twenty men behind him. He was determined to crush any opposition to Vermont's being a state before Clinton could bring in an outside force. Again the hills rang with the old war cry, "We're going on a big wolf hunt!" As of old the Green Mountain Boys came swarming out of farms, trappers' cabins, sawmills. In a short time Ethan had more than a hundred men behind him.

The Boys soon rounded up thirty-six leading pro-Yorkers and Tories in Putney, Brattleboro and other infected areas. Ethan locked them up in the jail at Westminster. He explained to the angry prisoners that he had arrested them in order to show Governor Clinton that he was not afraid of him. Ethan wanted a final showdown with the powerful state of New York. Then he seized a large quantity of ammunition which New York had sent in for an armed uprising.

A few days later the prisoners were brought to trial. Thumbing through his law book by Blackstone, the judge seemed unable to find any sound legal charges against them. He had quashed the indictments against the first three and was passing on to the fourth prisoner when suddenly the door of the courtroom banged open. Down the center aisle strode Ethan with his cocked hat and his big sword clanking at his side.

"What goes on here?" he roared.

He marched up to the bench, glowered at the judge and turned on the state's attorney, a young man who was paling visibly at the spectacle of Ethan's wrath.

"I would have the young gentleman know," Ethan thundered, while the courtroom vibrated with his voice, "that with my logic and reasoning from the eternal order of things, I can upset his Blackstones, his whitestones, his gravestones and his brimstones."

The judge was flabbergasted, but he had to maintain the dignity of his office. He informed Ethan that he would listen to him as a private citizen but not as an army officer.

Ethan accepted the rebuke. He tossed his cocked hat on the bench and, unbuckling his sword, laid it beside his hat. Then after quoting a couplet from Pope, he delivered one of his speeches.

"Fifty miles I have come through the woods with my brave men," he began, "to aid the sheriff and the court in prosecuting these Yorkers—the enemies of our noble state."

The judge and the spectators sat spellbound as Ethan roared out one flamboyant phrase after another. He demanded that the disloyal men be pun-

ished, that none should be permitted to escape
through some loophole in the law. When he had
finally ended, he reached for his sword, buckled
it on, jammed his hat on his head and strode out
of the room.

Whether it was the force of Ethan's personality, or the force of his eloquence that had an effect, it is hard to say, but at any rate the judge
changed his mind. He fined the rest of the accused
heavily and sent them off to New York. There
they told their sorrows to Governor Clinton.

Clinton was outraged by Ethan's conduct but,
like Tryon, he could do nothing but pick up his
pen and send a complaint to Congress. This had
become a habit among New York governors when
trouble occurred in the Grants. So now Clinton
wrote numerous letters to members of Congress
complaining about Ethan. He even sent one to
George Washington himself, asking the General
kindly to return the six brass cannon New York
had loaned the Continental army so that he could

blow the heads off Ethan and his riotous crew.

No one seems to have paid much attention to Governor Clinton's angry letters or his threats to blow off the heads of the Green Mountain Boys. Meanwhile, the Boys themselves returned to their ploughs and their sawmills with renewed admiration for their swashbuckling leader. As for Ethan, he soon became too busy trying to get Vermont recognized as a state to bother much about Clinton's official wrath.

Ethan had set his heart on forcing Congress to give Vermont statehood. And when Ethan set his heart on anything, he was apt to take extreme measures, sometimes at the expense of what might appear to be justice and moderation. He now began skating on thin ice, on ice so dangerously thin that the cry of treason was raised against him. In other words he began bargaining with the British.

The war was not quite over. Ten thousand British soldiers were still in Canada, able at any moment to invade Vermont. To the west lay New York, ready to absorb the infant state at the first chance. To the east was New Hampshire, ready to do the same. And far to the south in Philadelphia, Congress seemed not only indifferent to granting Vermont statehood, but actively opposed to it.

Ethan felt the situation was desperate and that only desperate measures would prevent his beloved state from being overwhelmed by her enemies. His plan was a simple one and followed his general tactics of threat, bluff and bluster. In order to keep the British from invading Vermont and at the same time force Congress to recognize her as a state, Ethan threatened to make a separate peace with England. As a rejected and fatherless child, Vermont had a right to do so, Ethan argued.

The British had secretly offered Ethan terms. Though it is unbelievable that a man who had suffered so much for his patriotism would betray his country, Ethan began playing a game with the enemy. He played his cards face up and in the open. "I do not hesitate," he wrote to the President of Congress, "to say I am fully grounded in opinion that Vermont has an indubitable right to agree on terms of cessation of hostilities with Great Britain, provided the United States persists in rejecting her application for a union with them."

Ethan's dealings with the British succeeded in keeping their army from invading Vermont, but they had less effect with Congress. Fortunately for everyone, the war came to an end. And though Vermont was not accepted as a state until long after, Ethan's dealings with the British ended when peace was made. The episode was not the brightest or noblest in Ethan's career.

There were others, however, in which he could play the role he starred in and one he enjoyed most. He was never so happy as when he was charging through Vermont at the head of his Green Mountain Boys, putting Yorker sheriffs to flight and keeping his state free and independent. Soon after the affair in the Westminster courtroom, Ethan had a chance to ride on a big wolf hunt again. This time it was in the direction of Guilford, which lay only forty miles east of Bennington.

For some years the town of Guilford had somehow managed to exist as a tiny province of New York. It boasted of its New York charter and when Vermont declared its independence in 1777, Guilford proclaimed its allegiance to New York. The citizens vowed that they were ready to resist the "pretended state of Vermont" with arms and started drilling openly on the village green.

Horrified Vermonters at once began calling for their champion, but Ethan was not around. He was off in Hartford overseeing the printing of a book he had written. A rider, sent posthaste by Governor Chittenden of Vermont, located Ethan and rushed him back to give the misguided citizens of Guilford one of his lessons in deportment.

Ethan gathered his Green Mountain Boys together. Then, mounted on a coal-black charger and in full military regalia, he started for Guilford. There were 250 men behind him. The first person the armed men encountered was Tim Phelps, a Yorker sheriff. He was brought to Ethan where he sat on his horse. Phelps at once began denouncing the Green Mountain Boys, calling them a pack of rioters and outlaws. Then, like so many Yorker sheriffs before him, he commanded them in the name of New York to disperse and return quietly to their homes.

During Phelps's speech Ethan, sword in hand, sat on his horse quietly listening. When Phelps had exhausted his fiery stream of adjectives and paused for breath in order to continue, Ethan leaned forward in his saddle. With one swipe of his sword he sent Phelps's hat spinning into a neighboring meadow.

"Take the blasted rascal out of the way!" he ordered. Then he dug his spurs into his mount and galloped toward Guilford.

He had gone only a short distance when he was met by some members of his advance guard. They told him excitedly that they had run into an am-

With a swipe of his sword he sent Phelps's hat spinning.

bush, been fired upon by some Guilford men, and that several of their men were lying bleeding on the ground.

History doesn't tell us what remarks Ethan made to his men who had fled from the enemy, but he swung down angrily from his horse and, brandishing his sword, marched alone toward the ambush. Reaching the crossroads where the Guilfordites lay hidden, he halted and gazed around him. Then, it is said, he roared out a challenge so that the very hills re-echoed with the sound of his voice:

"I, Ethan Allen, do declare that I will give no quarter to the man, woman or child who shall oppose me. And unless the inhabitants of Guilford peacefully submit to the authority of Vermont I swear that I will lay it as desolate as Sodom and Gomorrah, by God!"

The terrified Guilfordites sneaked out of their ambush and fled to their homes.

The Green Mountain Boys met no further opposition. Twenty or so Yorker sympathizers were

arrested and Ethan's army, now 400 strong, pro-
ceeded to Westminster where the prisoners were
lodged in jail. By this time the judge had learned
that it was Ethan and not Blackstone who was the
legal authority in Vermont. When the prisoners
were brought before him charged with treason,
insurrection and rebellion he needed no prodding
to give them all stiff sentences—heavy fines, jail or
banishment from Vermont with the confiscation
of their property.

This ended the last attempt of New York to
get a foothold in Vermont. It was Ethan's final
victory in a long and bitter war that he had won
without the loss of a single life.

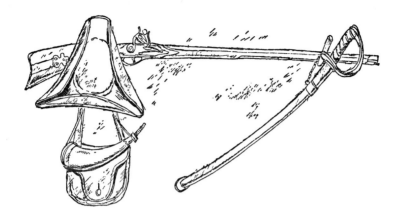

11

The Last Celebration

Ethan was growing old. He had grown old sooner than most men. The rugged life in field and forest, the thirty months of imprisonment with its hunger, cold, sickness, loneliness, the long nights in shackles, the aching hours in the rat-ridden, vermin-infested darkness of a ship's hold, the abuse, brutality, and privation had left their mark on him. Though his spirit flared when Vermont was in danger or when the old cry sounded across the hills, "We're going on a big wolf hunt!" the old fire was gone.

Gone, too, were many of his friends and some of his own family. During his imprisonment in New York he had lost his only son. Not long after he returned his wife, Mary, died. His brother Heman was dead and many of his old friends had gone, too. Remember Baker, as we have seen, had been killed and dozens of the Green Mountain Boys had lost their lives fighting the British.

A short while after he had buried Mary, Ethan married again. This time he took as a wife a gay widow twenty years younger than himself. Then with his three daughters and his new wife, Fanny, he moved to Burlington, far off in the wilderness of northern Vermont. There he sold out his rights in the Onion River Land Company to his brother Ira and built himself a house with the proceeds. The proceeds weren't large.

As has been stated earlier, the Onion River Land Company never brought Ethan and his brothers much profit. All the Allens died poor and Ira, who was the moving spirit in the venture, died a bankrupt.

If Ethan was interested in property, he was interested also in property for others. He was interested also in the right of a free man in a free country to own the land he lived on and the right, too, of handing it on to his children. "Life, Liberty and Property" was what interested Ethan. And he detested any way of life that denied land to the small farmer. He hated Yorkers not as individuals but because they represented an un-American system of living.

From the time he was a youth, Ethan had defended the American way of life against the feudalism of old Europe. With skill and courage he had fought the landowning system that the great proprietors of New York tried to impose upon

175

the Grants. Some of these men owned more than a million acres of land. Ethan fought them with every weapon at his command, but it was his native wits that won the battle. His shrewd tactics of threat, bluster and bluff kept the Grants free of redcoats and bloodshed and won the final victory for Vermont.

Ethan did not live to see the final victory himself. He never lived to see Vermont join the sisterhood of states. It was not until 1791, two years after Ethan had died, that Congress, overcoming the bitter opposition of New York, granted Vermont statehood. Up to the very end, Ethan had fought for Vermont's acceptance as a state, but during his last years he fought not with his old sword but with his pen. He wrote much and published numerous pamphlets and books. Except for his *Narrative of My Captivity*, no one reads them today.

But Ethan had taken pleasure in writing them.

With his light-hearted Fanny and his children to keep him company, he lived quietly, writing his pamphlets and tending his farm on the banks of the Onion River. It was a peaceful life and might have been a long one. But one bitterly cold night in February, Ethan suddenly died.

With a team of oxen and an old Negro servant, he had gone across the ice to South Hero Island to fetch a load of hay his cousin Ebenezer had promised him. Ethan's appearance anywhere was reason enough for a celebration and Cousin Ebenezer called in some of the Green Mountain Boys to talk over old times.

The party lasted late. It wasn't until early morning that Ethan and his faithful Negro servant crawled aboard the load of hay and started back across the frozen lake. A bitter wind was blowing and the runners of the sledge were shrill on the protesting snow. The old Negro, goading the patient oxen along, suddenly realized that Ethan had remained silent for too long a time. He glanced back over his shoulder. Ethan in his great coat lay staring lifeless at the stars.

He was buried with military honors. Drawn swords lay across his coffin as the funeral procession, to the sound of muffled drums, moved along the snow-packed road to the cemetery. Once every minute the procession paused while a brass cannon was fired in Ethan's honor. Then in gently falling snow the hero of Vermont was lowered into his grave.

There is no contemporary portrait of Ethan

Ethan died on the way home from a party.

Allen in existence, so we cannot tell exactly what he looked like. We do know that he was tall, broad-shouldered and powerful, with strong white teeth. In any case, it was Ethan's personality that counted and he left the mark of it everywhere in Vermont. And the Green Mountains themselves, not bleak or spectacular like other mountains, but warm and friendly, will ever stand like ancient witnesses to Ethan's wise and friendly heart.

Index

Index

fort built by, 81-82
on "gods of the hills," 15-16
Green Mountain Boys organized
    by, 18, 20-21
height of, 11
and Hough, Justice, 87, 95-96
land-jobbing charged against,
    126, 129
as leader of the Grants, 75
letter to Trumbull, 118-19
mock proclamation by, 57-59
money raised for war, 104
New York defied by, 54-56, 93,
    161-64, 169-72
newspaper articles by, 75-77
as prisoner of war, caning threat-
    ened, 133-34
    Dace pursued by, 139
    in England, 140-43
    exchange of, 151
    gifts from Irishmen, 144-46
    ill treatment of, 137-40, 148
    invitation to captain's table, 151
    in irons, 135, 137-39
    letter to Congress, 142
    life threatened, 132
    parole of, 151
    prisoners' lives saved by, 134-
    135
    return to America, 143-52
    and scurvy, 148-50
    trip to England, 139-40
proclaimed outlaw, 57
property-owning, views on, 39,
    175
reading by, 38
remarriage of, 174
reply to Captain Delaplace, 116
return to Bennington, 153-55
reward offered for capture of,
    69-70, 92
rifle used by, 101

settlers of the Grants defended
    by, 10-11, 13-15, 75-77
sisters of, 37
and Spencer, Benjamin, 85-89, 91
strength of, 11
surrender to British, 131
Ticonderoga captured by, 116-19,
    121
Vermont defended by, 161-64,
    168-72
Vermont statehood urged by,
    165-67
and war with England, 102-19,
    121-25, 130-31
and Washington, George, 152
wife of, first, 20, 41, 174
    second, 174, 177
Yorker surveyors punished by,
    45-46
See also Green Mountain Boys
Allen, Heman, 22, 37, 125, 156, 174
Allen, Ira, 37, 125, 127, 129, 174
American way of life, 7-8, 175
Arnold, Benedict, 106-08, 110-11,
    115, 117-18, 129

Baker, Remember, 21, 46, 53, 57,
    69, 96, 101, 123, 127
death of, 156
kidnaping of, 60-62, 64-65, 89
Baum, General, 157-59
Benedict, Landlord, 59
Bennington, Vermont, 10, 16, 26,
    33-34
Battle of, 156-60
Catamount Tavern in, 22
celebration of Ethan's return to,
    153-55
negotiations with Tryon, 68-69
Boston Tea Party, 40

Index

Index

Schuyler, General, 130
Scurvy, 148-49
Solebay, 144-47
Spencer, Benjamin, 84-91
Stark, General, 158
Sunderland, Peleg, 21, 95

Ten Eyck, Sheriff, 24, 26-31
Ticonderoga, Fort, *see* Fort Ticonderoga
Tories, 77, 160-61
Townships, sale of, 8-9
Trumbull, Governor, 118
Tryon, Governor William, 51-52, 55-56, 65-67
  British troops requested by, 80, 94
  Ethan proclaimed outlaw by, 57
  negotiations with the Grants, 68-69
  reward offered for Ethan's capture, 69-70, 92
  and Spencer, Benjamin, 84, 89
  as Tory, 147
"Twigs of the wilderness," 45-46

Vermont, 4, 154-55, 160
  constitution of, 156
  Ethan's defense of, 161
  Ethan's mark on, 179
  independence declared by, 168
  statehood granted to, 176
  statehood urged by Ethan, 165-66

Warner, Seth, 21, 69, 89-90, 95-96, 101, 107, 109, 117, 123
  in Battle of Bennington, 156, 158-160
  at Continental Congress, 124
  as lieutenant colonel, 125
Warren, Gideon, 22
Washington, George, 152, 164
Whippings, by Green Mountain Boys, 45-46, 96
Wing, Mehitabel, 19-20

Yale College, 38
Young, Dr., 38-40, 156

LANDMARK BOOKS

★

Have you read these World Landmarks?

★

CHECK THE LIST BELOW